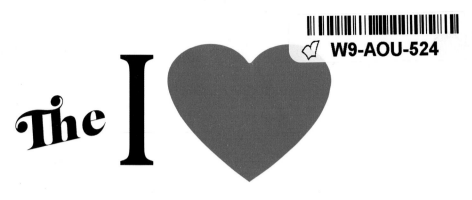

The I ♥ TRADER JOE'S© COOKBOOK

10TH ANNIVERSARY EDITION

Delicious Recipes Using Favorite Ingredients from the Greatest Grocery Store in the World

CHERIE MERCER TWOHY

ULYSSES PRESS

Published by:
Ulysses Press
P.O. Box 3440
Berkeley, CA 94703
www.ulyssespress.com

ISBN: 978-1-64604-528-0

Printed in China
10 9 8 7 6 5 4 3 2 1

Project editor: Keith Riegert
Managing editor: Claire Chun
Editor: Lauren Harrison
Proofreader: Renee Rutledge
Front cover design: Rebecca Lown
Interior design and production: what!design @ whatweb.com
Cover artwork: woman, corner edges, blue frame, utensils from envato and remaining images from shutterstock.com—pattern © mis-Tery; pasta © Bodor Tivadar; cauliflower © Nikolayenko Yekaterina; cupcake © bioraven
Interior photographs © Cherie Mercer Twohy except pages 44, 69, 84 © Judi Swinks/judiswinksphotography.com
Interior illustrations from shutterstock.com: background pattern pages 10, 24, 37, 46, 58, 65, 71, 81, 89, 102, 112 © mis-Tery; pages 14, 42, 45, 59, 64, 66, 91, 94 © Elena Pimonova; pages 16, 115 © NAtaLima; pages 30, 31, 53, 75, 77, 82, 86, 95, 100, 103, 104, 111 © Nikiparonak; page 38 © bioraven; pages 40, 52, 56, 126 © Yevheniia Lytvynovych; page 47 © lynea; pages 63, 70 © Babich Alexander; pages 90, 93, 99 © Olga_Zaripova; page 108 © Varlamova Lydmila; pages 110, 123 © Natalya Levish; page 113 © Alena Kaz; page 119; pages © Sketch Master; page 128 © Patrice Dwyer www.imagesbypatrice.com

CONTENTS

Chapter 4
BEANS, RICE, GRAINS, AND POTATOES 46

Chapter 5
POULTRY. 58

Chapter 6
BEEF AND LAMB 65

Chapter 7
PORK 71

Chapter 8

SEAFOOD 81

Chapter 9

PASTA. 89

Chapter 10

VEGETABLES 102

Chapter 11

DESSERTS 112

INTRODUCTION

Before I owned a cooking school, whenever I had friends over for drinks or dinner, they'd ask me, "Where did you get this fabulous cheese?" or, "What's that great spread?" Almost always, the answer included the magic words "Trader Joe's." This happened so frequently that friends even started asking to go to Trader Joe's with me because they had trouble finding the great stuff I loved. It was a bit embarrassing. After all, I did spend a couple years in culinary school. Nevertheless, many of the recipes that turned heads seemed to originate at the same store.

Once I opened Chez Cherie cooking school, I started offering classes featuring Trader Joe's products. I even asked our local store captain if he'd come spend a few minutes answering students' questions about how the stores select products, how they keep the prices so low, and how they can sell that wine for two bucks! I was always surprised to see how far students had traveled to attend class! That told me there was a lot of interest in the stores and their products. Of course, I like to think that even though we were not affiliated with them, we were doing some positive outreach for Trader Joe's in the process, since we truly loved what they do and appreciated all their great products and prices.

I've always been a huge fan of all the great stuff at Trader Joe's, but even now I tend to get tunnel vision in the stores. Let's face it, there is a lot going on in those stores! The aisles are sometimes narrow, the signage is wild and crazy, and the shelves are tightly stocked with colorful packaging. Especially when we're short on time, I think we all tend to zero in on the ingredients we need right away and filter out all the other stuff. But the other stuff is such fun! It's great to go to the stores when you aren't in a hurry and just stroll the aisles looking at what's interesting, new, and delicious.

I'm such a fan of Joe's that I visit three locations regularly. In fact, I find it helps get me inspired to visit a different TJ's store from time to time because the layout is always a little different from my home Joe's. This forces me to look with new eyes, and I tend to notice items I haven't seen before. Since I love to play with ingredients, this is great inspiration for creating menus! Try hitting up a new Joe's when you are in a different neck of the woods. Heck—I even head there when I'm on vacation! Who has better beach or poolside snacks than Trader Joe's? And after-ski or hiking munchables? I may just have to put together a tour of all 500-plus TJ's locations. Road trip!

When I was approached to write this cookbook, I was thrilled, of course, but it also seemed like a daunting task. After all, different Trader Joe's stores carry different items; there are regional and seasonal differences; and things do tend to go in and out of stock. Also, I didn't want to do a cookbook that consisted of "Open carton A, stir in contents of package B." I acknowledge that in our busy lives there is a time and place for that kind of food. I also think that the Trader Joe's cartons and packages are filled with better ingredients and fewer additives, preservatives, and artificial ingredients than those at most other stores. But I wanted us to really cook together. So, while you will find some very simple, stir-together recipes in this book, there are more ideas for actual cooking than for heating up a Trader Joe's pizza.

My hope for this book is that it will serve as inspiration and that the recipes will be jumping-off points for your own brilliant ideas on what to do with that terrific stuff at our favorite place to shop. Please view these recipes as templates, and let your imagination and taste buds suggest other flavor pairings for that rice dish or those palmiers. After all, new products are arriving at your Joe's every week. I'd love to hear your versions of these dishes, and I'm sure I'll be inspired by your changes and additions. You can brag to me at cherie@ilovetraderjoes.com. In the meantime, c'mon, let's go to Joe's!

WORKING YOUR JOE'S:
STRATEGIES FOR GETTING THE BEST OUT OF YOUR TRADER JOE'S® EXPERIENCE

- **MAKE FRIENDS WITH YOUR "JOES."** It's easy to do because they are friendly by nature. When I visit a TJ's, I often pay attention to the crew, and they are nearly always smiling, chatting, and offering help. Frequently, I'll pass a crew member in the aisle, and he or she will ask, "Can I help you find something?" (Not sure whether I look particularly helpless, but it's still nice.) I have overheard crew members deftly handle some very difficult customers with aplomb; they really do aim to please. Once you've established a relationship, your friends at TJ's will alert you to new stuff they think you might like. If you need something in quantity, call ahead, and they'll set it aside for you—not that they wouldn't do that anyway, but it's just more like dealing with a mom 'n' pop merchant if you are on a first-name basis.

- **CHECK OUT THE WEBSITE.** There's been a terrific improvement in the Trader Joe's website in the past few years: tons of dietary information, new product blurbs, and even recipes. (Hey! That's my job!) If there's a recall on an item, you can read about it not only at the checkout counter, where signs are posted, but also on the website. You can also read about TJ's lore, find store locations, and even talk back to Joe! E-mail your questions or fill TJ's in on your joys (at a new product that has rocked your world) or sorrows (I can't live much longer without the Hot and Sweet Mustard!). I've been told by Trader Joe's insiders that they do take customer requests very seriously, so let 'em know what you're thinking.

- **HOARD YOUR FAVORITES.** Hoarding is an ugly word, but sometimes ya gotta. Most of us have experienced the Heartbreak of TJ's when that staple ingredient, be it mustard, pie crust, or a particularly delicious mojito sauce, suddenly disappears from the shelf, leaving devoted customers feeling bereft. I've been shopping at Trader Joe's so long that I've been down this Heartbreak Road many, many times. So now, when I find some new shelf-stable or freezable item that I fall in love with, I purchase two or three. I use those and replace them as I do, so I've always got a couple in reserve in case there's a supply problem and my TJ's is out for a week or two. I also watch the shelves for signs of change. If my favorite salsa usually has a "four-jar-across" placement and I notice that it has diminished to two, I get nervous. I'll see if I can find out why it's in short supply, and if I can't, I'll grab a few extra jars, just in case.

- **GO TO "THE ALTAR."** The folks up there know stuff. Rather than ask a crew member who's stocking shelves about a product, head up to the front desk and ask someone there. They have access to a computer list that will give you the straight scoop on whether something is held up at a port of entry (which happened during the Great Caper Shortage of '08), or TOS (temporarily out of stock), or the dreaded DISCONTINUED. If something you love and need has been (horrors!) given the big "D" (and it is a sort of divorce, sometimes—painful and sudden, and you feel helpless and alone), ask for the flyer that contains addresses and phone numbers for all the TJ's locations. Zero in on the ones in your "willing to drive there" zone and call them. (I am a little embarrassed to admit that I have more than two TJ's on my speed dial.) If they have some of your beloved item in stock, they'll hold it for you.

- **THINK OUTSIDE THE FROZEN-FOOD BOX.** Just because it says frozen carrots doesn't mean you can't use it in a million ways. Think about the ingredient, not the finished product. Don't look at that frozen brown rice just as a microwavable side dish—think of it as a head start on fried rice (using up the remnants of several bags of frozen veggies and the last egg in the carton), or as an add-in to make leftover soup heartier and more healthful.

- **WATCH THE DISPLAYS FOR NEW ITEMS AND "HUSTLE BUYS."** This is a good way to find a great new snack or salad dressing or grab a terrific bottle of Hustle Buy wine or beer at a fantastic price before it's going-going-gone.

- **VISIT INSTAGRAM.** Check the helpful Instagram account @traderjoestobediscontinued for helpful heads-ups.

- **SUBSCRIBE TO THE TJ'S PODCAST.** Binge-listen (and subscribe to) the podcast Inside Trader Joe's for insight into many aspects of TJ's, both on the shelves and behind the scenes.

- **LISTEN TO OTHER CUSTOMERS AND ASK QUESTIONS.** Trader Joe's is a friendly place, so they will probably be happy to help. If you see someone putting eight boxes of curry sauce in her cart, ask what fabulous dish she has in mind. Not only will you get a great recipe idea, you might also make a friend. After all, you have a discerning appreciation of Trader Joe's in common.

Chapter 1

STARTERS, SMALL PLATES, NIBBLES, AND NOSHES

Personally, I could live on a steady diet of snacks from Trader Joe's! Crackers and cheeses alone would sustain me for weeks. Then there are the spreads, dips, and a rainbow of hummuses (hummi?) to liven up anything from crudités to pitas.

The nut section is jammed with fresh and interesting blends, spiced and candied nuts, and all manner of trail mixes and dried fruits. One of the many things I love about TJ's is that the nut section has such quick turnover. That's important, because nuts are full of oil, which makes them taste great, but it also means they can go rancid pretty quickly. A rancid nut is not a pretty thing. For that reason, I always try to buy nuts where the turnover is high so I know that the nuts are fresh and haven't been sitting on the shelf all season. I store nuts in the freezer so they stay fresh longer and then toast them in a dry sauté pan to reactivate those flavorful oils before use.

One of my hands-down favorite TJ's items of the past few years is the utterly fabulous frozen All Butter Puff Pastry. Why do I love it so much? For one thing, it's flat, not folded like a letter. This makes much more sense for puff pastry, because the cracks that inevitably ensue when you unfold it are not as easily repaired as with, say, pie crust. Also, it's made with butter instead of hydrolyzed what-have-you. Let's face it—puff pastry is not a health food, so I say go for the glorious taste and texture that butter brings to the party, and diet tomorrow. This puff pastry is better than any commercial pastry I've ever found, and even better than puff pastry I made myself, from scratch, back in my overachieving culinary-school days. Pick a spread or tapenade off the shelf, slather it on a sheet of defrosted puff, roll or cut the pastry into serving sizes, bake it, and you're almost guaranteed a winning appetizer. Toss a handful of cheese or chopped nuts on there, and you're a culinary genius. I get really nervous if I have fewer than five boxes of this frozen treasure on hand. The frozen puff pastry is stocked seasonally, so my advice is to seriously hoard the stuff. If they ever discontinue this … well, I simply can't contemplate that tragedy.

From simple to stellar, the recipes in this section are designed to get your creative juices flowing (and your mouth watering). Making a meal of appetizers, tapas-style, is my favorite way to eat and also to entertain. Whether you are making one quick nibble or an impressive array of hors d'oeuvres, I hope you'll add these to your repertoire.

CHERRY CROSTINI with PECORINO ROMANO

So simple, so pretty, so unusual. What more do you need from a 10-minute appetizer? The Trader Joe's Cherry Preserves are marvelously chunky, which is perfect for these little bites of wonderful.

1 loaf of artisan-style bread (I love the Trader Joe's Organic Whole Grain Loaf)
1 (17.5-ounce) jar Trader Joe's Cherry Preserves
freshly ground black pepper
Pecorino Romano cheese, for garnish

VEGETARIAN

Preheat the oven to 400°F or use a toaster oven. Slice the bread into ¼-inch slices. Spread each slice with some of the cherry preserves. Generously season with black pepper. Place on a baking sheet and warm in the oven, 4 to 6 minutes. Using a vegetable peeler, shave several swaths of Pecorino Romano over the warm crostini.

SERVES: About 20 servings per loaf
PREP TIME: 5 minutes
COOKING TIME: 4 to 6 minutes

Try some toasted and chopped walnuts or pine nuts sprinkled on top.

NO PEANUT "PEANUT" SAUCE

This is a great solution for those who crave Thai flavors but can't have peanuts. The taste is close to my favorite take-out noodles.

3 cubes frozen garlic
1 cube frozen ginger
1 tablespoon sriracha
¼ cup soy sauce
¼ cup rice vinegar
2 tablespoons brown sugar
2 teaspoons sesame oil
¼ cup Trader Joe's Mixed Nut Butter

VEGETARIAN

Combine all ingredients in small saucepan and bring to a bubble over medium heat. Stir until smooth.

SERVES: 4, with a pound of noodles
PREP TIME: 3 minutes
COOKING TIME: 5 minutes

Serve over long, thin pasta, rice, shrimp, or chicken.

ROASTED APRICOTS with HONEYED GOAT CHEESE

We used this recipe in several Aphrodisia cooking classes when I ran a cooking school. Sexy and delicious, the soft flesh of the apricot pairs beautifully with the tangy cheese. The whisper of heat from the hot sauce should induce a very slight lip tingle.

4 lusciously ripe apricots, halved and pitted (if apricots are not in season, use plump, plush dried ones)

4 ounces soft, fresh goat cheese, such as Trader Joe's Chèvre, Madame Chèvre, or Silver Goat Chèvre

small splash of Trader Joe's Chili Pepper Sauce or Jalapeño Pepper Hot Sauce

2 tablespoons honey

1 tablespoon pistachios, coarsely chopped

VEGETARIAN, GLUTEN-FREE

Preheat the broiler. Fill the hollows of the apricots with mounds of goat cheese. Arrange on a baking sheet and place under the broiler for 2 to 3 minutes, until slightly browned. Remove from heat. Stir a drop or two of the hot sauce into the honey and drizzle the spiked honey over the apricots. Sprinkle with chopped pistachios.

SERVES: 4
PREP TIME: 5 minutes
COOKING TIME: 3 minutes

TSAO NUTS

These spicy-sweet beauties are great in salads, as a garnish for savory dishes, or to simply gobble by the handful!

⅓ cup Trader Ming's General Tsao Stir Fry Sauce

2 tablespoons honey

2 cups pecans

freshly ground black pepper

VEGETARIAN

Preheat the oven to 300°F. Line a baking sheet with a silicone baking mat or parchment. In a large bowl, mix the General Tsao sauce and honey and then stir in the pecans to coat well. Arrange in a single layer on the lined baking sheet and bake, stirring once or twice, for 35 to 45 minutes, until the nuts are well-coated and the sauce has formed a glaze. Remove from the oven and sprinkle with freshly ground black pepper. Cool slightly before removing from the baking sheet, and break into pieces.

MAKES: 2 cups
PREP TIME: less than 5 minutes
COOKING TIME: 45 minutes or less

ARTICHOKE and BASIL SPREAD

This is a really versatile spread. I love to make garlic bread with it, or use it as a pasta sauce or a pizza topping. My favorite "dippers" for this spread are Trader Joe's Lowfat Rye Mini Toasts.

large handful of basil leaves
1 (12-ounce) bag frozen Trader Joe's Artichoke Hearts, defrosted
2 cubes frozen crushed garlic
¼ cup Greek or Mediterranean plain yogurt
squeeze of lemon juice
pinch of red chile pepper flakes or a shake of hot sauce (to taste)
½ cup grated Parmesan cheese

VEGETARIAN, GLUTEN-FREE

In a food processor, chop the basil leaves roughly. Add the artichoke hearts and garlic cubes and chop coarsely. Add the yogurt, lemon juice, red chile pepper flakes or hot sauce, and Parmesan cheese, and process to desired consistency (chunky or smooth). Adjust seasoning to taste.

SERVES: 4 to 6
PREP TIME: 5 minutes
COOKING TIME: none

THESE LITTLE PIGGIES

Adorable sliders in a flash. Put a platter of these in front of a crowd of sports fans, and they'll disappear faster than a two-point lead. Better make a triple batch.

8 Trader Joe's Mini Hamburger Buns, or other rolls (see note)
1 (16-ounce) container Trader Joe's Pulled Pork in Smoky BBQ Sauce
about ½ cup Trader Joe's Corn and Chile Tomato-Less Salsa
1 ripe avocado

Slice the buns horizontally and toast them, if desired, in a toaster oven or under the broiler in a regular oven. Heat the pork according to package directions. Pile 2 to 3 tablespoons of the pork on each bun and top with a tablespoon of salsa. Add a slice of avocado and finish with the top of the bun.

SERVES: 4
PREP TIME: 5 minutes
COOKING TIME: 5 minutes

If the hamburger buns aren't available, use Trader Joe's Brioche Buns, Panini Rolls, or Focaccia Bread, cut into two-bite pieces.

BAKED CAMEMBERT
with HONEY and HAZELNUTS

A rustic bistro appetizer in the blink of un oeil. This is a simple but oh-so-French presentation that's perfect for a picnic, even if it's on the coffee table. Très bon.

1 round (about 250 grams or 9 ounces) Trader Joe's Camembert or another creamy, soft cheese

2 tablespoons flavorful honey

2 tablespoons chopped hazelnuts (or other nuts)

sliced baguette or crackers, and/or sliced apples or pears

VEGETARIAN, GLUTEN-FREE (IF GLUTEN-FREE CRACKERS OR FRUIT ARE USED)

Preheat the oven to 350°F. Remove the cheese from the box, unwrap, and cut off the top rind. (Don't throw it away—that's the "cook's treat"!) Place the cheese back in the box, drizzle the honey over the top, and scatter the chopped hazelnuts on top. Place on a baking sheet and bake until the cheese is warmed, about 12 to 15 minutes. Serve with a baguette or crackers, or sliced fruit.

SERVES: 4 (or just me)
PREP TIME: 5 minutes
COOKING TIME: 15 minutes

The Camembert in the adorable stapled wooden box is a holiday item, so if it's not in stock, try this with another creamy cheese. Just put it in a small, ovenproof baking dish. Don't try this with a glued box—the oven heat will melt the glue and you will have a gooey, if delicious mess on your hands (or your baking sheet).

ASPARAGUS, PROVOLONE, and PROSCIUTTO INVOLTINI

Emily Post grants permission to eat asparagus with one's fingers. By all means, do so with these irresistible treats. The combination of the nutty asparagus, gooey cheese, and salty, rich pork is a winner.

12 asparagus spears, about pencil thickness

6 slices provolone

12 slices prosciutto or Trader Joe's Black Forest Ham

GLUTEN-FREE

Preheat the oven to 400°F. Trim the stem end of the asparagus, place the spears on a baking sheet, and roast for 6 to 8 minutes, until nearly tender (but not floppy). Remove from the oven and cool slightly.

Cut each provolone slice in half. Starting with the cut edge, roll a slice of cheese around each asparagus spear. Don't worry if it cracks and breaks a little—the prosciutto will hold everything together.

Wind a slice of prosciutto around the cheese-wrapped spear (in a spiral) and place on the baking sheet again. Repeat with the remaining ingredients. Return the baking sheet to the oven and bake until the cheese is slightly melted, about 5 minutes.

SERVES: 4 to 6
PREP TIME: 15 minutes
COOKING TIME: less than 15 minutes

Involtini simply means one thing rolled inside another. These are also great with the jarred artichokes with stems. Substitute the stemmed beauties for the asparagus—you may want to cut them in half, from tip to stem.

APPLE SAUSAGE and CHEDDAR BITES

Yeah, they're kinda pigs in blankets. But really tasty pigs in wonderful, flaky eiderdowns.

1 sheet Trader Joe's All Butter Puff Pastry, defrosted but kept cold

about 2 tablespoons Dijon mustard

½ cup grated sharp cheddar cheese

2 Trader Joe's fully cooked Smoked Apple Chardonnay Chicken Sausages

Preheat the oven to 400°F. On a lightly floured board, slightly roll the puff pastry, if necessary, to about ¼-inch thickness. (Roll from the center toward the edges, but try not to "clunk" the rolling pin over the edges, as it will compress the dough and inhibit the flaky layers from puffing.)

Cut the pastry in half. Spread a little mustard over the surface of each piece of pastry, leaving the edges clean. Sprinkle half the grated cheese over the surface of the pastry, leaving the edges clean. Place a sausage at one long edge of one of the pieces of pastry and roll up the pastry to encase it completely. Repeat with the second sausage and pastry.

Place on a baking sheet and bake until the pastry is golden, about 18 minutes. Cool slightly before cutting into 1-inch pieces with a serrated knife.

SERVES: 4
PREP TIME: 10 minutes
COOKING TIME: less than 20 minutes

Don't limit yourself to one type of sausage with this recipe. TJ's has about a dozen flavors of these precooked flavor bombs, so try the Trader Joe's Sweet Apple Chicken Sausage, or the Smoked Andouille Chicken Sausage, or any of the other great combinations.

GREEN OLIVE and GORGONZOLA PALMIERS

These crispy treats are great as an appetizer or with a bowl of soup. The Trader Joe's frozen puff pastry is high on my "desert island" list. It's the best puff I've ever worked with, including homemade, which is not something that happens often in my life!

1 sheet Trader Joe's All Butter Puff Pastry, defrosted but kept cold

½ (10-ounce) jar Trader Joe's Green Olive Tapenade

½ cup crumbled Trader Joe's Crumbly Gorgonzola Cheese (or another easily crumbled, not-too-wet cheese)

VEGETARIAN

Preheat the oven to 400°F. On a lightly floured board, slightly roll the puff pastry, if necessary, to about ¼-inch thickness. (Roll from the center toward the edges, but try not to "clunk" the rolling pin over the edges, as it will compress the dough and inhibit the flaky layers from puffing.) Spread the tapenade over the dough, leaving a small border clean on all sides.

Scatter the Gorgonzola evenly over the surface, and gently press in with the palms of your hands. Starting with one long edge, roll up the dough fairly tightly in a spiral fashion toward the center. Repeat with the other long edge until the two spirals meet in the center. With a sharp knife or bench scraper, cut crosswise slices about ½-inch thick.

Place the palmiers on a parchment-lined baking sheet. If the dough seems soft, chill in the freezer for 10 minutes. Bake until puffed and golden, about 18 minutes.

SERVES: 6
PREP TIME: 10 minutes
COOKING TIME: less than 20 minutes

There are tons of possibilities here—try the Trader Joe's Roasted Red Pepper and Artichoke Tapenade with some grated Parmesan cheese, or the Trader Joe's Eggplant Garlic Spread with a little feta cheese, or maybe the Trader Joe's Red Pepper Spread with Eggplant and Garlic. You'll come up with your own terrific flavor-popping creations once you see how easily these come together and what a great "wow" factor they generate!

ASPARAGUS TART

I loved a clipping of this recipe that I found in the Los Angeles Times *food section about a decade ago. I lost the tattered newsprint version a while back but have been making it by heart ever since. This is a great spring appetizer or brunch dish. You can get very "Type A" and line up all the spears with the points in one direction, or you can do my preferred tumbled look.*

2 teaspoons butter or olive oil

1 onion, thinly sliced

1 sheet Trader Joe's All Butter Puff Pastry, defrosted but kept cool

1 cup grated Gruyère or smoked Gouda

1 (12-ounce) package asparagus

handful of chopped hazelnuts or other nuts (optional)

zest of 1 orange or lemon

VEGETARIAN

Preheat the oven to 400°F. In a medium sauté pan, heat the butter or olive oil and sauté the onion over medium-high heat until slightly softened, about 10 minutes. Set aside to cool to room temperature.

On a lightly floured board, slightly roll out the puff pastry, if necessary, to about ¼-inch thickness. (Roll from the center toward the edges, but try not to "clunk" the rolling pin over the edges, as it will compress the dough and inhibit the flaky layers from puffing.) Transfer to a parchment-lined baking sheet. Scatter the grated cheese over the pastry, leaving about a ½-inch edge clean on all sides. Fold the pastry up to make a "picture frame" or score the edge with a knife or fork to make it pretty. Top with the sautéed onion.

Place the asparagus in a single layer on top, cutting to fit if necessary. Bake until pale golden, about 18 to 20 minutes if not using nuts. If using nuts, scatter them over the surface of the tart after it has baked 15 minutes and return the tart to the oven for about 5 more minutes. Remove from the oven and sprinkle the zest over the top. Cut into squares to serve.

SERVES: 4 to 6
PREP TIME: 15 minutes
COOKING TIME: 20 minutes

The I ♥ TRADER JOE'S® COOKBOOK

MEATBALL SPIEDINI with OVOLINE

Kids of all ages love these colorful kabobs. They have a polka-dot look that's just pure fun. Carry the dotted theme further by halving some large tomatoes, placing them cut-side-down on a platter, and sticking the skewers in for display. You can scatter extra cherry tomatoes and mozzarella balls on the plate, too.

1 (20-ounce) bag Trader Joe's Party Size Mini Meatballs, defrosted or still frozen

1 (25-ounce) jar Trader Giotto's Organic Vodka Sauce (or another tasty pasta sauce)

about 40 fresh basil leaves, rinsed

1 (16-ounce) container Trader Joe's Mixed Medley Cherry Tomatoes or 1 pound heirloom tomatoes, cut in wedges

short bamboo skewers or long toothpicks

1 (8-ounce) container Trader Joe's Ovoline or Ciliegine mozzarella in lightly salted water

GLUTEN-FREE

Simmer the meatballs in the sauce until cooked through (which will take longer if they are still frozen) and coated with sauce. Wrap a basil leaf around a meatball and pierce with a bamboo skewer, securing the basil leaf in place. Top each meatball with a wedge of heirloom tomato or a cherry tomato, a piece of mozzarella, and another tomato. (If you are using the ovoline, cut it in marble-sized pieces.) Finish with another basil leaf. Repeat with the remaining ingredients to create more spiedini.

SERVES: 4 to 6
PREP TIME: 15 minutes
COOKING TIME: less than 10 minutes for thawed meatballs, less than 20 for frozen

"Spiedini" means skewers in Italian. "Ciliegine" means cherry, and it's a great name for these little cherry-sized mozzarella balls. Perfectly shaped for popping in your mouth, they are great for this dish or for scattering in a salad or on a pizza.

EGGSADILLAS

Ever since I first visited Austin, Texas, I've been enamored with the concept of breakfast tacos. Really, why are these not more of a thing? A breakfast burrito is fine, but they are usually pretty massive affairs, leaving me feeling as stuffed as a burrito long past lunchtime. One morning, I was heading in a breakfast taco direction, when I noticed that my small, street taco–sized tortillas were just about the perfect size for a fried egg. My first eggsadilla was born.

2 tablespoons grapeseed oil, divided

4 eggs

8 small white corn tortillas

1 cup shredded Mexican cheese blend

Trader Joe's Jalapeño Pepper Hot Sauce, or jalapeño sauce or salsa of choice

sliced avocado (optional)

VEGETARIAN

In a medium nonstick sauté pan, heat 1 tablespoon of the oil and fry 2 eggs until just set, with a runny yolk. Remove from pan and drain on a paper towel. Repeat with the remaining eggs and remove from pan to the towel.

Assemble eggsadillas: Place one tortilla on a flat surface. Top with about 2 tablespoons of cheese, a squiggle of jalapeno sauce, and an egg. Place a couple slices of avocado (if using) on top of the egg, and sprinkle another 2 tablespoons of cheese on top. Place another tortilla on top. Add a little more oil to the pan and heat over medium-high heat.

Fry the first eggsadilla while assembling the second. Flip the first eggsadilla over and fry on the second side. Repeat with the remaining eggsadillas.

SERVES: 4
PREP TIME: 10 minutes
COOKING TIME: 15 minutes

You probably don't need me to tell you, but these breakfast treats are a perfect vehicle for many additional ingredients. Carnitas, roasted chiles or vegetables, cooked potatoes—the list is endless. Just keep that yolk runny, because, in my mind, that's one of the most delicious sauces there is.

Chapter 2

SALADS

I remember waaaay back when TJ's carried very little fresh produce. The produce section has expanded over the years, and they now sell many items (apples and squash, for example) individually. They introduced an initiative to reduce their packaging in the product area, and are really doing a better job of eliminating plastics and increasing the use of alternative packaging on things that require containers. Individual blueberry sales proved problematic! During the holidays, they even carry pomegranate arils, the ruby-colored seeds inside those leathery casings, which can be murder to remove. When my kids were little, we had a neighbor who liked to "gift" them with these delicious, healthful, but incredibly messy fruits. I would only let them eat the fruit naked, in the bathtub, to avoid indelible stains on T-shirts and under fingernails! So, when I first saw that little jewel box of preseeded glory, I couldn't believe my good fortune! I think I thanked Joe right out loud.

The packaged salads and mixed greens are mostly triple-washed, although I confess to rewashing them myself. I'm not sure I'm eradicating anything with my extra rinse, but it makes me feel proactive, and I think it refreshes the greens at the same time. To ensure the liveliest possible greens, be vigilant about checking expiration dates, and use them within a day or two of purchase.

The oil and vinegar section at TJ's is small but mighty, with an assortment of high-quality olive oils in manageable sizes. Let's face it: It's no bargain to purchase a gallon of olive oil if you use only about a pint a month. Olive oil does not improve with age, and if you use just half of it before it goes rancid, you've wasted the money you meant to save by buying in bulk. I love the Trader Joe's California Estate Olive Oil. Why not decrease the food miles and enjoy those delectably oily fruits that are grown in California? This oil is unfiltered and made with Arbequina olives, which have a buttery top note with a hint of pepper at the back of the throat. I especially appreciate the dark-tinted bottle—it filters out some ultraviolet rays, which hasten the spoilage of oils. Another favorite is the Spanish olive oil. Any time I'm doing tapas, this is my go-to oil.

TJ's generally has a couple of interesting vinegars on the shelf—one of my favorites is the Orange Muscat Champagne Vinegar. This is a customer success story, as it was discontinued but brought back by popular demand. I still mourn the discontinuation of the amazing Pomegranate Vinegar. That stuff was so fragrant, I was always tempted to dab some on my pulse points! Of course, being the TJ's hoarder that I am, I have a treasured half bottle in reserve. But Joe, how 'bout bringing that one back? The red wine vinegar is good quality, and their balsamics, though far from the $150-a-bottle elixirs found in gourmet outlets, are fine for adding some depth of flavor to a vinaigrette or sauce. One of my favorite tricks is to pour a whole bottle of the stuff into a saucepan and reduce it by at least half. This will concentrate the flavor and give it a syrupy consistency that's great with roasted meats or over poached pears or strawberries. If I happen to have a leftover vanilla bean lying around, I'll stick that in the jar with the reduced balsamic. It just adds a little secret something.

I love to put a dab of mustard in a vinaigrette because it adds flavor and helps keep the dressing from separating into an oil layer and a vinegar layer. That little dollop of spicy mustard will help the salad emulsify temporarily when you give it a vigorous shake or whisk. I'm working through the last of my hoarded jars of the fabulous TJ's Hot and Sweet Mustard, which they discontinued. JOE! You done me wrong here, and I am mounting a campaign to bring this glorious elixir back! In the meantime, I've recommended Dijon mustard in the dressing recipes, but if the beloved Hot and Sweet Mustard returns, by all means, use that. The Honey Pale Ale Mustard is pretty great, too.

Whether salad is a side dish or the showpiece of the meal, you'll find great inspiration for ingredients on Joe's shelves. A handful of nuts or dried fruit, a crumble of savory cheese, and a whisk of freshly made vinaigrette, and you've created a masterpiece of healthful goodness.

NECTARINE, GORGONZOLA, and GREENS

Nectarines are my favorite fruit, and for the brief period that they're perfect, I could eat them at every meal. Here's a way to sneak them onto the lunch or dinner table, where their golden glow will perk up your spirits.

1 (7-ounce) bag arugula

2 ripe nectarines (or peaches), cut into wedges

¼ red onion, thinly sliced

¼ cup Trader Joe's Crumbled Gorgonzola Cheese

¼ cup toasted walnuts

1 tablespoon red wine vinegar

2 teaspoons Dijon mustard

3 tablespoons olive oil

salt and freshly ground black pepper

VEGETARIAN

Arrange the arugula on a platter. Place the nectarine wedges around the platter. Scatter the sliced red onion, crumbled Gorgonzola, and walnuts over the salad. Whisk together the vinegar and mustard, then, whisking continuously, add the olive oil in a thin stream. Taste the dressing on a leaf of arugula and adjust seasoning with salt and pepper. Lightly dress the salad and serve.

SERVES: 4
PREP TIME: 10 minutes
COOKING TIME: none

Try adding grilled steak strips, cooked chicken, or roast pork to this.

The I ♥ TRADER JOE'S® COOKBOOK

SWEET POTATO, PECAN, and CRANBERRY SALAD

The vibrant, earthy orange of the sweet potatoes paired with the deep red of the cranberries is so pretty that this is a dish you'll definitely eat with your eyes. Full of antioxidants, this salad is both gorgeous and good for you.

1 sweet potato, cubed

drizzle of olive oil

1 tablespoon Dijon mustard

1 teaspoon honey

2 tablespoons red wine vinegar

⅓ cup olive oil

1 (5-ounce) bag Trader Joe's Herb Salad Mix or Baby Spring Mix salad greens

½ cup candied pecans

handful of dried cranberries or cherries

handful of crumbled feta or blue cheese

salt and pepper

VEGETARIAN

Preheat the oven to 425°F. Toss the sweet potato cubes with olive oil, salt, and pepper. Place in a single layer on a baking sheet and roast until tender, about 20 minutes. (Or use leftover roasted sweet potatoes for this purpose.) In a small bowl, whisk together the mustard, honey, and vinegar. Stream in oil, whisking constantly. Toss the greens with a little dressing and arrange on a platter. Scatter the candied pecans and cranberries or cherries over the greens and top with roasted sweet potatoes. Drizzle with a little more dressing and garnish with crumbled cheese.

SERVES: 4
PREP TIME: 10 minutes
COOKING TIME: 20 minutes

ALL-ABOUT-TJ'S SALAD

This is one of those "add and subtract" salads. Don't like beets? You can leave 'em out. (But please, won't you try them? They taste nothing like the ones from a can!) If you prefer blue cheese, skip the goat cheese and scatter crumbled Gorgonzola or Maytag blue on top. Got some leftover roast chicken? Great—toss that in, too!

½ cup pepitas (roasted pumpkin seeds)

1 (5-ounce) log goat cheese (Trader Joe's Chèvre, Madame Chèvre, or Silver Goat Chèvre)

½ (4-ounce) bag Trader Joe's Baby Spring Mix

½ (7-ounce) bag arugula

1 (8-ounce) box Trader Joe's precooked Baby Beets, cubed (in the salad and vegetable section)

handful of dried cherries

DRESSING:

2 teaspoons Dijon mustard

drizzle of honey (optional)

2 tablespoons Trader Joe's Orange Muscat Champagne Vinegar

⅓ cup canola or grapeseed oil

salt and pepper

VEGETARIAN, GLUTEN-FREE

Chop the pepitas coarsely (with a knife or in a food processor). Put the chopped seeds on a cutting board or parchment sheet and roll the log of goat cheese in the seeds to coat thoroughly. Set aside.

In a small bowl, whisk together the mustard (and honey, if using) and vinegar. Drizzle in the oil, whisking constantly. Adjust seasoning to taste with salt and pepper. Dress the greens very lightly and arrange on salad plates.

Dress the beets with a little more of the dressing and scatter over greens. Cut the seed-coated goat cheese into ½-inch-thick rounds and place a slice atop each salad. Scatter dried cherries on top.

SERVES: 4
PREP TIME: less than 10 minutes
COOKING TIME: none

Dental floss works great for cutting the goat cheese—just make sure to use the plain version, not the minty-fresh!

AVOCADO, ORANGE, and OLIVE SALAD

The creaminess of avocado pairs so well with the tang of citrus, and the olives bring salt and a counterpoint of color. This is a great addition to a tapas-party menu.

2 ripe avocados, sliced lengthwise

2 oranges, peeled and sliced into wheels

1 cup pitted black or green olives

DRESSING:

juice of 2 limes

2 tablespoons olive oil

pinch of ground cumin

VEGAN, GLUTEN-FREE

Arrange the avocado slices and orange wheels on a plate. Scatter the olives over the top. Whisk together the lime juice, olive oil, and cumin. Drizzle over salad.

SERVES: 4
PREP TIME: less than 10 minutes
COOKING TIME: none

If you make this in winter, when blood oranges are in season, the colors will make you swoon with pleasure.

WARM MUSHROOM SALAD

A study in autumn tones, the creamy, warm mushrooms create an amazingly lush dressing for the greens. This salad is among the most popular recipes we ever presented at my cooking school. Students still tell me they use it all the time for entertaining. Nothing could make me happier!

2 ounces bacon or pancetta chopped

1 shallot, thinly sliced

8 ounces fresh mushrooms, cleaned and sliced (I like a mix of crimini, shiitake, and portabella.)

2 tablespoons red wine vinegar

½ (7.5-ounce) container crème fraîche

1 (5-ounce) bag mixed baby greens, such as Trader Joe's Baby Spring Mix or Herb Salad Mix

handful of shredded carrots

salt and pepper

GLUTEN-FREE

Sauté the bacon or pancetta over medium-high heat in a medium sauté pan until beginning to crisp, about 3 minutes. Add the shallot and sauté another minute, until fragrant. Add the sliced mushrooms and reduce heat to medium. Continue to sauté for 5 to 6 minutes. (At first, the mushrooms will absorb the bacon drippings and will appear dry. After a few minutes, they will release some of their juices and will appear moister. At this point, they will begin to soften and cook.) Season the mushrooms with salt and pepper as they cook.

When the mushrooms are tender, add the vinegar and cook for 2 minutes. Add the crème fraîche and warm through. Adjust seasonings to taste. Arrange the greens on a platter and scatter shredded carrots over them. Top with the warm mushrooms. They'll wilt the greens slightly, and the sauce will dress the greens.

SERVES: 4
PREP TIME: 15 minutes
COOKING TIME: less than 15 minutes

A slice of bacon is about an ounce, so two will do nicely for this recipe. You might want to cook an extra for the cook's treat!

CARNE ASADA SALAD

This is a one-dish meal salad full of spice and crunch. It's pretty enough to serve when guests are expected but quick enough to throw together before soccer practice.

1 (5-ounce) bag Trader Joe's Herb Salad Mix

1 tablespoon olive oil

1 pound Trader Joe's Carne Asada Auténtica, thinly sliced

2 tablespoons red wine vinegar

½ (13.75-ounce) jar Trader Joe's Corn and Chile Tomato-Less Salsa

1 avocado, sliced

½ red onion

handful of Trader Joe's Mixed Medley Cherry Tomatoes

¼ English cucumber, thinly sliced

salt and pepper

GLUTEN-FREE

Arrange the greens on a platter. Heat the olive oil in a large sauté pan and sauté the meat over medium-high heat until rare. Remove the meat from the pan and arrange over the greens. Add the vinegar to the pan and heat through. Tumble the corn salsa, avocado, red onion, tomatoes, and cucumber on top of the meat and season to taste with salt and pepper. Drizzle the hot vinegar over the salad.

SERVES: 4
PREP TIME: 10 minutes
COOKING TIME: less than 10 minutes

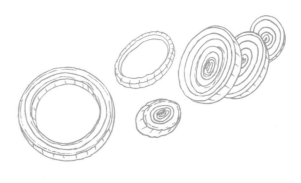

SAUSAGE and SPUDS SALAD

Another meat-and-potatoes salad that is great for tailgating or game-watching. While I lack the sports gene, I'll root for any team that's serving this on the sidelines!

1 pound fingerling, red, or Trader Joe's Teeny Tiny Potatoes

2 tablespoons olive oil

2 cubes frozen crushed garlic

1 red onion, cut into slivers

1 (12- to 12.8-ounce) package cooked Trader Joe's Sun-Dried Tomato Chicken Sausage, Smoked Andouille Chicken Sausage, or another precooked sausage you like, cut into 1-inch pieces

3 tablespoons red wine vinegar

1 tablespoon Dijon mustard

⅓ cup olive oil

1 bag baby spinach (or other salad greens)

GLUTEN-FREE

Preheat the oven to 425°F. Cut the potatoes into quarters if they are large or in half if they are small. Toss the potatoes with the olive oil, garlic, and red onion. Arrange in a single layer on a rimmed baking sheet and roast until the potatoes are nearly tender, about 15 minutes. Add the sausage pieces and roast for another 10 minutes, until sausage is warmed through and starting to brown.

While the vegetables (and sausage) cook, whisk together the red wine vinegar and mustard. Drizzle in the olive oil, whisking constantly. When the vegetables and sausage are cooked, toss them with all but two tablespoons of the vinaigrette. Toss the spinach (or salad greens) with the remaining vinaigrette. Arrange the leaves on a platter or individual plates and top with the roasted vegetables and sausages.

SERVES: 4
PREP TIME: 10 minutes
COOKING TIME: 25 minutes

ASIAN FLAVORS SLAW

This slaw is great on its own, but I especially love it with some leftover roasted pork tenderloin or roasted chicken on top. Shrimp works, too!

3 cups shredded green cabbage

1 cup shredded carrots

1 red bell pepper, cut into thin strips

2 green onions, shredded

¼ cup cilantro, coarsely chopped

1 tablespoon canola oil

1 tablespoon toasted sesame oil

2 tablespoons soy sauce

1 tablespoon rice vinegar

2 teaspoons brown sugar

1 jalapeño, minced

2 cubes frozen crushed garlic

1 teaspoon minced ginger

VEGETARIAN, GLUTEN-FREE

In a large bowl, toss together the shredded cabbage, carrots, red bell pepper, green onions, and cilantro. Whisk together the two oils, soy sauce, rice vinegar, brown sugar, minced jalapeño, garlic, and ginger. Toss the salad with the dressing and arrange on a platter.

SERVES: 4 to 6
PREP TIME: 10 minutes
COOKING TIME: none

ARUGULA, CHICKEN, and WALNUT SALAD

Most chicken salads are mayo-intensive, but this one is light on its feet, with a hot vinaigrette to perk it up. This is great for lunch with friends or a summer supper when it's too hot to heat up the oven.

½ (7-ounce) bag arugula

⅓ cup olive oil, divided

1 pound boneless, skinless chicken (breast or thigh), cut into bite-sized pieces

1 cup red bell pepper strips

3 tablespoons red wine vinegar

½ cup walnut pieces

2 teaspoons rosemary, chopped

Parmesan cheese, for garnish

GLUTEN-FREE

Arrange the arugula on a serving platter. Heat 2 tablespoons of the olive oil in a large sauté pan and sauté the chicken pieces over medium-high heat until nearly cooked through, about 5 minutes. Add the red bell pepper strips and sauté an additional 2 to 3 minutes, until tender. Add the vinegar and sauté until bits of food stuck to the bottom of the pan release. Pour the pan contents over the arugula. In the same pan, heat the remaining olive oil and add the walnuts and rosemary. Sauté until fragrant, about 3 minutes, and pour over the chicken. Shave Parmesan cheese on top, as desired.

SERVES: 4
PREP TIME: 15 minutes
COOKING TIME: less than 10 minutes

PUMPKIN and CARNITAS SALAD

I like to make this as soon as there is a nip in the air. It looks and tastes like October! If you ask me, we don't eat nearly enough pumpkin. Break out of the pumpkin pie rut and discover the joys of roasted pumpkin. It has become one of my favorite fall vegetables.

1 small pie pumpkin

1 red onion, thinly sliced

about 5 tablespoons olive oil, divided

½ (7-ounce) bag arugula

½ (10-ounce) bag red or green cabbage

1 tablespoon red wine vinegar

¾ (12-ounce) package Trader José's Traditional Carnitas

Asiago or Parmesan cheese, for garnish

salt and pepper

GLUTEN-FREE

Preheat the oven (convection, if available) to 425°F. Wash the pumpkin and cut off the four "cheeks," so that all you have is the pumpkin meat, leaving the seeds and strings behind. Cut the quarters into 1-inch crescents and remove the skin, if desired.

Toss the pumpkin pieces and red onion slices in about 2 tablespoons of olive oil, and season with salt and pepper. Place on a baking sheet and roast until soft and beginning to caramelize, about 18 minutes. Remove and set aside.

Combine the arugula and cabbage in a bowl and toss with the red wine vinegar and remaining olive oil. Arrange greens on a platter or individual plates. Top with roasted pumpkin and red onion.

Microwave the carnitas for 3 minutes or sauté over medium-high heat for 5 minutes, until it reaches desired doneness. Shred or chop and scatter over the salad. Shave Asiago or Parmesan cheese over the salad, and serve.

SERVES: 4
PREP TIME: 15 minutes
COOKING TIME: less than 20 minutes

You won't use all of the carnitas for this salad, so there'll be leftovers for a taco or two. The salad is delicious without the carnitas, too—but you'll have to change the name of the recipe!

GRILLED FLATBREAD SALAD

The flatbread forms an edible plate to hold the crisp greens and the tangy dressing. The vinaigrette flavors the pizza-style crust, making a crunchy treat. The fun presentation makes this salad a winner at any table. Look for the pizza dough with the prepared salads and sandwiches, not in the frozen foods section.

1 pound Trader Joe's Pizza Dough (Plain, Whole Wheat, or Herb and Garlic)

1 tablespoon red wine vinegar

1 teaspoon Dijon mustard

3 tablespoons olive oil

1 (5-ounce) bag salad greens, such as Trader Joe's Baby Spring Mix or Herb Salad Mix

1 ripe avocado, sliced

¼ English cucumber, sliced

½ red onion, sliced

handful of Trader Joe's Mixed Medley Cherry Tomatoes

VEGETARIAN (IF NO MEAT IS ADDED)

Preheat a grill to high heat and brush grates with a brass-bristled brush to clean well. Form the pizza dough into 4 to 6 rustic rectangles. When the grill is hot, place the dough on the grill and cook until grill marks are visible and the dough is set on the bottom, about 3 minutes. Flip the dough over and cook on the second side until crisp, another 2 to 3 minutes. Set aside.

Whisk together the red wine vinegar and mustard. Drizzle in the olive oil, whisking as you do so. Toss the salad greens with a little bit of the dressing and arrange on top of the grilled flatbread. Arrange the remaining ingredients on top of the greens and drizzle with more dressing.

SERVES: 4
PREP TIME: 10 minutes
COOKING TIME: less than 10 minutes

If protein is desired, add ¼ to ½ pound sliced grilled flank steak, tri-tip, or pork tenderloin, cooked shrimp, or Trader Joe's Just Chicken.

CRUNCHY SESAME SALAD
with CHARRED MANDARINS

I love the look of the charred citrus—it seems like a fancy restaurant move but only takes a few seconds to achieve. The sugars caramelize super fast and add an extra level of flavor.

1 (7-ounce) bag Trader Joe's Butter Lettuce & Radicchio

2 Persian cucumbers, sliced

½ red onion, thinly sliced

2 mandarin oranges, peeled and sliced into rounds

handful of sesame sticks or honey sesame almonds

Trader Joe's Organic Toasted Sesame Dressing

VEGETARIAN

Preheat the broiler. In a salad bowl, combine the lettuce, cucumbers, and red onion. Place the mandarin slices on a baking sheet and broil, watching carefully, until they are charred in spots. Turn with a spatula and repeat. Add to the salad. Add the sesame sticks and dress lightly with Toasted Sesame dressing.

SERVES: 4 to 6
PREP TIME: 5 minutes
COOKING TIME: 5 minutes

I'm not much for bottled dressings—I love to shake up a fresh vinaigrette based on the salad of the day's ingredients. But this toasted sesame stuff is really delish—not only for salads. I use it to marinate chicken thighs, pork, and shrimp. Any of those, cooked, would be great in this salad.

Chapter 3

SOUP

"Beautiful, beautiful soup" sang Lewis Carroll's Mock Turtle, and I echo his ode to this simple, satisfying meal in a bowl. At Trader Joe's, there are premade soups in the salad and sandwich refrigerated case, and there are soups in the frozen case. A big bowl of frozen French onion soup, complete with cheese, is a great mood elevator on a stormy day! There are soups in round-bellied cans and soups in shelf-stable Tetra packs. There are soups that are satisfying on their own and soups that beg to be gussied up.

My favorite items on the soup front are the premade broths, from which a quick soup can be made in moments. The rectangular containers of chicken, vegetable, and beef broth are ready to go. There are 4 cups of broth in each package, and the sodium content is reasonable, compared to canned broth (or stock) or bouillon cubes.

The newest additions to the broth arena are refrigerated organic broths and stocks of various descriptions. Vegetable, chicken, or beef—they are a useful shortcut in lieu of simmering your own. Of course, that's a satisfying project on occasion, too. Get your soup on, however you choose. TJ's ingredients make it easy.

CREAMY TOMATO and ROASTED RED PEPPER SOUP with PESTO GNOCCHI

This soup can be made in the time it takes to read the recipe through once. The pillowy gnocchi are soft in the mouth, and the pesto adds great color and flavor. Plus, it's so pretty and satisfying, you'll make it over and over.

1 (32-ounce) container Trader Joe's Tomato & Roasted Red Pepper Soup

4 ounces mascarpone

⅓ (6.17-ounce) package potato gnocchi

about 4 tablespoons Trader Giotto's Pesto alla Genovese (in the refrigerated case)

salt and pepper

VEGETARIAN

Heat the soup, then stir in the mascarpone. While the soup heats, bring a small pot of water to a boil. Add the gnocchi and boil just until they bob to the surface, 3 to 4 minutes. Scoop them out and set aside. Season the soup to taste with salt and pepper, ladle into bowls, and add a few gnocchi to each serving. Drizzle a little pesto into each serving.

SERVES: 4
PREP TIME: 5 minutes
COOKING TIME: 10 minutes

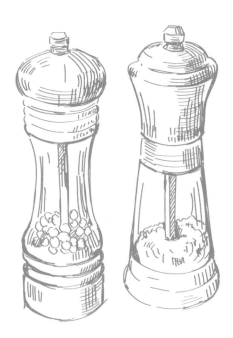

THANKSGIVING in a BOWL

Some TJ's ingredients are seasonal, but many are shelf-stable, so you can stockpile the ones you love. The fried onion pieces will crunch up casseroles, salads, and even sandwiches, so grab a few before they disappear with the holidays!

1 (32-ounce) container Trader Joe's Sweet Potato Bisque or Butternut Squash Soup

1 (7.5-ounce) container crème fraîche

2 tablespoons bourbon

2 ounces smoked turkey breast, cut into slivers

about ¼ cup Trader Joe's Gourmet Fried Onion Pieces

salt and pepper

In a medium saucepan, warm the soup with the crème fraîche and bourbon. Season to taste with salt and pepper, and garnish with slivers of turkey and a few fried onion pieces.

SERVES: 4
PREP TIME: 5 minutes
COOKING TIME: 10 minutes

POTSTICKER SOUP

When I feel a cold coming on, I set a pot of this soup on the stove to simmer. It may not be a cure, but at least psychologically it does the trick. The steam seems to clear my head, and the warming broth makes me feel comforted, as soup always does.

4 cups chicken or vegetable broth

1 tablespoon rice vinegar

1 tablespoon soy sauce

2 cubes frozen crushed garlic

½ (16-ounce) package frozen chicken or vegetable potstickers (about 12)

1 (20-ounce) bag stir-fry vegetables

½ cup shredded carrots

4 green onions, thinly sliced

2 teaspoons sesame oil

VEGETARIAN (IF VEGETABLE BROTH AND VEGETARIAN POTSTICKERS ARE USED)

In a medium saucepan, combine the broth, rice vinegar, soy sauce, and garlic. Bring to a boil. Add the potstickers and bring back to a boil. Reduce heat and simmer for 4 minutes. Add the stir-fry vegetables and carrots and simmer until vegetables are tender and potstickers are cooked through, about 3 minutes. Garnish with green onions and a drizzle of sesame oil.

SERVES: 4 to 6
PREP TIME: 5 minutes
COOKING TIME: 15 minutes

HEARTY SHERRIED MUSHROOM SOUP

This soup is rich and creamy, but without a ton of cream. Using both fresh and dried mushrooms brings a silken texture and a deep, smoky flavor to the bowl.

4 tablespoons butter, divided

2 shallots, finely chopped

1 pound fresh mushrooms (crimini, button, shiitake, portabella, or a combination), finely chopped

2 tablespoons flour

1 tablespoon dried mushroom powder made from ½ (.88-ounce) package Trader Joe's Mixed Wild Dried Mushroom Medley (see note)

4 cups vegetable broth

3 tablespoons dry sherry

salt and pepper

crème fraîche, for garnish

VEGETARIAN

In a medium saucepan, melt 2 tablespoons of butter and sauté the shallots over medium-high heat until fragrant, 3 to 4 minutes. Add the chopped mushrooms and sauté until the mushrooms release their liquid and appear a bit dry, about 5 minutes. Remove to a bowl and set aside.

In the same saucepan, melt the remaining butter. Add the flour and stir into a paste. Cook over medium-low heat until the flour loses its bleachy aroma, about 3 minutes. Add the dried mushroom powder. Stir to incorporate and cook another minute. Add the sautéed mushrooms and broth, and bring to a boil. Reduce heat, salt and pepper lightly, and simmer for 20 minutes. Add the sherry and adjust seasonings to taste. Swirl in a little crème fraîche for garnish.

SERVES: 4 to 6
PREP TIME: 5 to 10 minutes
COOKING TIME: 30 minutes

To make the mushroom powder, grind the dried mushrooms in a coffee grinder until powdered. These are also great for coating fish fillets before roasting or sautéing. The intense, smoky taste adds great flavor.

ALMOST-FROM-SCRATCH BUTTERNUT SQUASH SOUP with BOURBON

This squash soup tastes like it was an all-day project but comes together in a snap, especially if you use the packages of precut squash in the produce section. Be sure to get really fresh ones (check the expiration date), as squash keeps a long while in its whole state, but once it's cut, it becomes quite perishable. Buy it only one or two days before you use it, at most.

1 tablespoon olive oil

1 large red onion, chopped

2 pounds butternut or acorn squash, peeled and cut into 1-inch cubes

1 russet potato, peeled and cut into 1-inch cubes

4 cups chicken or vegetable broth

2 tablespoons bourbon

2 tablespoons heavy cream (optional)

pinch of red chile pepper flakes

salt and white pepper

VEGETARIAN (IF MADE WITH VEGETABLE BROTH), VEGAN (IF MADE WITH VEGETABLE BROTH AND NO CREAM), GLUTEN-FREE

Heat the olive oil in a stockpot, and sauté the red onion over medium-high heat, about 5 minutes. Add the squash, potato, and broth, and bring to a boil. Add a pinch of salt, reduce heat to low, cover, and simmer until vegetables are soft, about 20 minutes. Purée, preferably using an immersion blender. (To purée in a food processor, strain, reserving liquid and solids, and purée solids carefully, adding reserved liquid as necessary. Return to stockpot and add remaining liquid until desired consistency is achieved.) Add bourbon and cream (if using), and adjust seasoning to taste with salt, white pepper, and red chile pepper flakes.

SERVES: 6 to 8
PREP TIME: 10 minutes
COOKING TIME: less than 30 minutes

Whole squashes are carried seasonally at TJ's, but you can get the precut cubes in the fresh vegetable section nearly year-round.

POTATO-KALE MINESTRA

The sausages are precooked, but sautéing them in the oil adds irresistible color and transmits some of their flavor to the oil, which then carries it throughout the soup. On a cold day, a steaming bowl of this is heaven.

1 tablespoon olive oil

½ pound Trader Joe's Smoked Andouille Chicken Sausage, cut into ½-inch slices

1 onion, diced

2 cubes frozen crushed garlic

1 tablespoon fresh rosemary, minced

1 pound russet potatoes, cubed

rind of Parmesan cheese (optional)

4 cups chicken or vegetable broth

2 cups chopped kale (bagged) or Trader Joe's Southern Greens Blend

salt and pepper

grated Parmesan cheese, for garnish

GLUTEN-FREE

Heat the olive oil in a medium saucepan and sauté the sausages over medium-high heat until browned, about 4 minutes. Set the sausages aside. In the same pan, sauté the onion until fragrant and softened, 5 to 6 minutes. Add the garlic and sauté until fragrant, about 2 minutes. Add the rosemary, potatoes (and Parmesan rind, if using), and broth. Bring the liquid to a boil, reduce the heat, and simmer for about 10 minutes. Add the sausage and simmer until the potatoes are tender, about 10 minutes. Add the Southern Greens Blend or kale and simmer until it is wilted and tender, about 5 more minutes. Season to taste with salt and pepper. (Remove the rind, if used.) Ladle into bowls and pass the grated cheese for garnish.

SERVES: 4 to 6
PREP TIME: 10 minutes
COOKING TIME: less than an hour

EZO GELIN (DAUGHTER-IN-LAW LENTIL SOUP)

I loved everything about our culinary trip to Turkey—the people, the culture, the landscapes, and the food. At our hotel in Istanbul, there was a piping cauldron of lentil soup in the lobby after 10 p.m. Such a comforting thing to put in your belly before sleep! I also understand it can prevent a hangover, not that I'd know anything about that. Legend has it that a Turkish newlywed created the recipe to win over her skeptical mother-in-law.

¼ cup butter

1½ cups finely chopped red onion

2 tablespoons tomato paste

½ cup Trader Joe's Red Split Lentils

4 cups beef stock (chicken or vegetable broth or water can be used)

1 teaspoon dried mint or 1 tablespoon fresh mint, minced

1 teaspoon red pepper flakes

salt and pepper

smoked paprika

In a medium saucepan over medium heat, melt the butter and sauté the onion until translucent, 3 to 4 minutes. Add the tomato paste, stir to coat the onions, and sauté for another minute. Add the lentils and stock. Bring to a boil, reduce the heat, and simmer for 30 minutes, until the lentils are tender. Season with mint, red pepper flakes, salt, pepper, and smoked paprika. Simmer for 5 minutes.

SERVES: 4 to 6
PREP TIME: 5 minutes
COOKING TIME: 40 minutes

If you like a brothier consistency, you can add more stock or water as you add the seasoning.

CHILE and CRAB CHOWDER

Rich and satisfying, with some heat to wake and shake those taste buds, this soup is a bowlful of creamy, crabby goodness.

2 tablespoons butter

1 medium onion, chopped

4 cups vegetable or chicken broth

1 medium boiling potato, cubed

1 teaspoon chopped fresh thyme

1 (4-ounce) can Trader Joe's Hatch Valley Fire-Roasted Diced Green Chiles

1 cup corn kernels, fresh or frozen

½ pound Jack's Premium Catch refrigerated canned crabmeat

½ cup half-and-half or heavy cream

½ cup grated sharp cheddar cheese

dash of Trader Joe's Chili Pepper Sauce or Jalapeño Pepper Hot Sauce

salt and pepper

GLUTEN-FREE

Heat the butter in a saucepan over medium-high heat, and sauté the chopped onion until it begins to soften, about 5 minutes. Add the broth, potato, and thyme, and bring to a boil. Reduce heat to low and simmer until potato is tender, about 15 minutes. Stir in the chiles and corn. Add the crabmeat and the half-and-half or cream, and warm through. Remove from the heat, stir in the grated cheddar cheese, and allow the heat of the chowder to melt the cheese. Season to taste with hot sauce, salt, and pepper.

SERVES: 4 to 6
PREP TIME: 5 minutes
COOKING TIME: less than 30 minutes

A boiling potato (labeled Trader Joe's Baby Red Potatoes, Dutch Yellow Baby Potatoes, or Potato Medley–Red, Gold, and Purple) has a thinner, smoother skin than a russet, or baking, potato. These babies will hold their shape better when simmered than a russet, which will tend to fall apart.

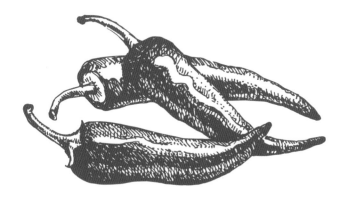

Chapter 4

BEANS, RICE, GRAINS, AND POTATOES

The grains section of Trader Joe's has a different selection of products almost every time I visit, so it's a fun place to experiment with new meal ideas. From plain white rice to several special mixtures, like the Harvest Grains Blend, the bags promise tasty meals or sides in the making. The ancient and very healthful quinoa is there to test your pronunciation skills—it's "keen-wha"—and it's practically a miracle food. Although it is treated as a grain, it's really a seed from a leafy plant similar to spinach, and it's a complete protein, so it's great for people limiting or eliminating meat from their diets. Quinoa's creamy, slightly nutty texture makes it super for salads and for serving alongside roasted or grilled meats. It's terrific for breakfast (think oatmeal) with some agave syrup drizzled over it or with a dollop of one of Trader Joe's excellent yogurts.

If cooking rice is your culinary Waterloo, or if time is just too short, TJ's carries precooked rice in several forms. The vacuum-sealed, shelf-stable wild rice is quite a time-saver, since wild rice can take 45 minutes to an hour to reach the toothsome tender state. One of the biggest sellers is the frozen rice. Now, I first heard about this when I overheard a customer complaining about it being out of stock. My snooty chef-brain (which lays low almost all the time but rears its ugly head on rare occasions) shot imaginary fireworks into the air. "Frozen RICE? Who is lazy enough to need frozen rice? That's only one step up from the plastic-wrapped russet potatoes at the grocery store, already prepped for the microwave." Luckily, this was internal monologue, so no one came to blows. Next time I was in the store, I checked it out and saw that not only did they have frozen white rice, they had frozen brown rice. Well now, that's an entirely different kettle of fish—or pot of rice! Brown rice, like wild rice, takes a long time to cook. Since I was looking to lose a few pounds, and brown rice is not only healthful but tends to fill me up fast, I was curious. Inside the gigantic cardboard box, there were three plastic-clad portions. Poke the obligatory hole, pop in the microwave, and a mere three minutes later, I had nutty, tasty, fluffy brown rice. A scoop of my beloved Corn and Chile Tomato-Less Salsa on top, and I had a zippy, tasty lunch that saw me happily through weeks of that dieting period. I can cook brown rice, of course, but it takes 40 minutes or more. Do you know how many Jelly Bellies I can eat in 40 minutes while waiting for that blasted brown rice to be done? Be sure to buy the frozen brown rice when you see it because it is hard to keep in stock.

The selection of grains at Trader Joe's is ever-evolving, and these bags of goodness keep well, so I try to visit that area of the store frequently and stock up on a bag or box of something new or an old favorite. Israeli couscous will keep a long while, and I never know if it will be going-going-gone from the aisle. Hoarding, people … not a pretty word, but it's part of the strategy of shopping at TJ's!

BLACK BEAN SALAD

This is a great make-and-take salad. For Music in the Park, seaside picnics, or just for brown-baggin' it, this salad is perfect because it's tasty cold or at room temperature.

2 (15-ounce) cans Trader Joe's Organic Black Beans, drained and rinsed

3 stalks celery, chopped

1 red onion, chopped

1 (¾-ounce) package fresh cilantro, chopped

1 teaspoon ground cumin

¼ teaspoon red chile pepper flakes, crushed

2 tablespoons Trader Joe's Orange Muscat Champagne Vinegar or red wine vinegar

1 teaspoon Dijon mustard

½ cup olive oil

salt and pepper

VEGAN, GLUTEN-FREE

In a medium bowl, combine the black beans, celery, red onion, and cilantro. In a separate bowl, combine the cumin, crushed red chile pepper flakes, vinegar, and Dijon mustard, then whisk in the olive oil and toss with the bean mixture. Season to taste with salt and pepper.

SERVES: 4 to 6
PREP TIME: 15 minutes
COOKING TIME: none

QUICK BLACK BEANS and RICE

So fast, so full of flavor. This is great as an accompaniment to any Latin-American or Spanish main dish, or simply folded into a warm tortilla. Pass the cheese, please!

1 tablespoon olive oil

2 cubes frozen crushed garlic

pinch of dried oregano

pinch of ground cumin

1 (15-ounce) can Trader Joe's Organic Black Beans, drained

juice of 1 lime

salt and pepper

3 cups cooked white or brown rice

2 tablespoons chopped cilantro (optional)

VEGAN, GLUTEN-FREE

In a medium sauté pan, heat the oil and sauté the garlic until fragrant, 2 to 3 minutes. Add the oregano and cumin and sauté another minute. Add the drained black beans and sauté to warm through. Remove from the heat and squeeze in the lime juice. Adjust seasonings to taste with salt and pepper, and mound on top of hot cooked rice. Garnish with cilantro, if desired.

SERVES: 4
PREP TIME: 5 minutes
COOKING TIME: 5 minutes

COUSCOUS with DRIED FRUIT

A little Mediterranean in flavor profile, this side dish gets its great texture from the dried fruit mixed with the fluffy couscous. And it's good for ya, too!

2½ cups chicken broth
1 cinnamon stick
¼ cup chopped dried cherries
¼ cup chopped dried apricots
generous pinch of salt
2 tablespoons butter
1 (17.6-ounce) box Trader Joe's Whole Wheat Couscous
salt and pepper

Place the chicken broth, cinnamon stick, dried fruits, salt, and butter in a medium saucepan, and bring to a boil. Stir in the couscous, cover, and remove from heat. Let stand for 5 minutes. Fluff with a fork. Season to taste with pepper and more salt, if needed.

SERVES: 4 to 6
PREP TIME: 10 minutes
COOKING TIME: 10 minutes

For a pretty presentation, butter a ramekin and pack the couscous mixture in, then invert onto a dinner plate to serve.

WILD RICE with SHIITAKES

There's something about combining rice and mushrooms that brings out the best of both. The earthy mushroom flavor brings depth to the fluffy, steamy rice grains. Any leftovers make a great snack the next day.

2 tablespoons butter
2 shallots, chopped
1 (3.5-ounce) package shiitake mushrooms, chopped
⅔ cup uncooked Trader Joe's Wild Rice
2 teaspoons fresh thyme leaves
2 cups beef broth (or chicken broth or water)
salt and pepper

VEGETARIAN (IF WATER IS USED), GLUTEN-FREE

In a medium saucepan, melt the butter and sauté the shallots and mushrooms over medium-high heat until softened, about 5 minutes. Set the vegetables aside. In the same saucepan, add the wild rice, thyme leaves, and broth. Bring to a boil. Reduce the heat, cover, and simmer for about 45 minutes, until the rice is tender and the liquid is absorbed. (Drain off excess liquid, if necessary.) Stir in sautéed mushrooms and shallots and adjust seasoning to taste with salt and pepper.

SERVES: 4
PREP TIME: 10 minutes
COOKING TIME: 1 hour

MUSHROOM HAZELNUT RICE

Add-ins are a great way to perk up a bowl of rice. The mushrooms and nuts bring such a satisfying earthiness to this dish, and the lemon zest makes it come alive.

1 tablespoon butter

1 tablespoon olive oil

1 cup fresh or frozen mushrooms, chopped

¼ cup hazelnuts, chopped

2 cubes frozen crushed garlic

4 cups cooked rice, or frozen rice, thawed

zest of 1 lemon

salt and pepper

VEGETARIAN, GLUTEN-FREE

Heat the butter and olive oil in a medium sauté pan. Add the mushrooms and sauté over medium heat for about 5 minutes. Add the hazelnuts and garlic and sauté until fragrant, 2 to 3 minutes. Add the cooked rice and warm through. Season to taste with salt, pepper, and lemon zest.

SERVES: 4 to 6
PREP TIME: 5 minutes
COOKING TIME: 10 minutes

ISRAELI COUSCOUS

I literally yelped with delight when I found Israeli couscous on the shelf at my Joe's. I love this roly-poly, nutty-flavored pasta-grain hybrid. It cooks quickly, looks great on the plate, and is a vehicle for any number of flavor combinations you might dream up. Israeli couscous? Yes!

2 tablespoons butter

½ red onion, chopped

1 (8-ounce) box Trader Joe's Israeli Couscous

2 tubes Trader Joe's chicken or vegetable Savory Broth concentrate

⅓ cup dried cranberries

½ cup pistachios, coarsely chopped

salt and pepper

VEGETARIAN (IF VEGETABLE BROTH IS USED)

In a medium sauté pan, melt the butter and sauté the onion over medium-high heat until tender, about 4 minutes. Add the couscous and sauté until golden, another 2 to 3 minutes. Add enough water to cover the couscous and pour in the broth concentrate. Add the dried cranberries and bring to a boil. Reduce heat and simmer, stirring occasionally, adding more water if the couscous becomes too dry, until the grains are tender, about 12 minutes. Season to taste with salt and pepper, and garnish with chopped pistachios.

SERVES: 2 to 3
PREP TIME: 5 minutes
COOKING TIME: 20 minutes

CITRUS and HARVEST GRAINS SALAD

Although I serve this on greens, it is so grain-based that I think it belongs in the grains chapter. With or without the greens, this dish is tasty and brimming with healthful goodness.

VINAIGRETTE:
3 tablespoons Trader Joe's Orange Muscat Champagne Vinegar

2 teaspoons Dijon mustard

½ cup olive oil

salt and pepper

SALAD:
1 (4-ounce) bag mâche (or other soft lettuce)

1 cup Trader Joe's Harvest Grains Blend, cooked according to package directions

1 blood orange (or regular orange), peeled and sliced

1 ruby grapefruit, segmented

1 ripe avocado, sliced

¼ English cucumber, sliced

VEGAN

FOR THE VINAIGRETTE: Whisk together the vinegar and mustard. While whisking vigorously, begin to drizzle in the olive oil, a little at a time. When the vinaigrette begins to thicken, add olive oil a little more at a time until all is incorporated. Taste on a leaf of lettuce, and adjust seasoning with salt and pepper.

FOR THE SALAD: Toss the greens with a little dressing and arrange on plates or a platter. Mound the cooked grains in the center of the platter, and drizzle on a little more dressing, reserving about two tablespoons of dressing. Arrange the citrus segments, avocado, and cucumber on the salad and drizzle with the remaining dressing.

SERVES: 4
PREP TIME: 5 minutes
COOKING TIME: 15 minutes

QUINOA with MINI-PEPPERS

Quinoa is an ancient grain from high in the Andes. Packed with nutrients, quinoa takes on flavors like tofu does, so the red pepper spread really shines in the dish. Quinoa is a great substitute for rice, and it's fun to say, too. KEEN-WHAAAA!

1 (16-ounce) box Trader Joe's Organic Quinoa

2 teaspoons olive oil or butter

6 sweet mini peppers, sliced into rings

¼ cup Trader Joe's Red Pepper Spread with Eggplant and Garlic (in a jar near the pastas)

salt and pepper, or Trader Joe's 21 Seasoning Salute

VEGETARIAN, VEGAN (IF OLIVE OIL IS USED)

Cook the quinoa according to package directions. While the grain cooks, heat the butter or olive oil in a small sauté pan, and sauté the pepper rings over medium-high heat until tender, 3 to 4 minutes. Set aside. When the quinoa is cooked, stir in the Red Pepper Spread. Top with sautéed pepper rings. Season to taste with salt and pepper or 21 Seasoning Salute.

SERVES: 4 to 6
PREP TIME: 5 minutes
COOKING TIME: 15 minutes

CHERRY RICE PILAF

This tasty side is a delight for the senses. The flavor of the dried cherries is deep, almost caramelly, and the walnuts add a toothsome crunch. The colors look great on a plate.

2 tablespoons butter

1 red onion, chopped

1 cup chopped celery

½ cup dried cherries

½ cup chopped walnuts

1 teaspoon dried thyme

3 cups cooked rice (white or brown), or frozen rice, defrosted

salt and pepper

VEGETARIAN, GLUTEN-FREE

In a medium sauté pan, melt the butter over medium heat. Sauté the red onion, celery, cherries, walnuts, and thyme until tender, about 8 minutes. Combine with the cooked rice, season with salt and pepper, and cook until heated through.

SERVES: 2 to 4
PREP TIME: 5 minutes
COOKING TIME: 10 minutes

Cook extra rice for dinner the night before to give yourself a head start on this dish, or use precooked rice from the freezer aisle.

ROASTED MUSHROOM POLENTA STACKS

These make a great vegetarian main dish or side dish. The Italian flavors are earthy and rustic, and the presentation is restaurant-worthy.

1 (18-ounce) roll Trader Joe's Organic Polenta (precooked), cut in ¼-inch rounds

2 portabella mushrooms

1 tablespoon olive oil

4 ounces fresh mozzarella, cut into ¼-inch rounds

1 (24-ounce) jar Trader Giotto's Rustico Pomodoro Pasta Sauce (or another tasty sauce)

1 roasted red pepper, cut into strips

several fresh basil leaves, chiffonaded

salt and pepper

VEGETARIAN, GLUTEN-FREE

Preheat the oven to 450°F. Place the polenta rounds on a parchment-lined baking tray. Toss the mushrooms with olive oil and season with salt and pepper. Place them on the baking tray and roast until mushrooms are tender, about 10 minutes. Slice into strips. Place a warmed polenta round on each plate and top with a slice of mozzarella and a dollop of pasta sauce. Drape some mushroom strips across the top and then some red pepper strips. Top with chiffonaded basil.

SERVES: 4
PREP TIME: 10 minutes
COOKING TIME: 10 minutes

SAFFRON POTATOES and PANCETTA

These are absolutely gorgeous and full of flavor. Another great tapa or a side dish perfect for roast chicken or fish.

½ pound fingerling potatoes, halved lengthwise

pinch of Trader Joe's Spanish Saffron

2 teaspoons balsamic vinegar

1 shallot, minced

2 tablespoons crème fraîche

½ cup chopped pancetta

salt and pepper

2 tablespoons Italian parsley, chopped

GLUTEN-FREE

Place the potatoes and saffron in a medium saucepan and cover with water. Bring to a boil, reduce heat, and simmer until tender, about 15 minutes. Drain the potatoes and toss with the balsamic vinegar. In a medium bowl, mix the minced shallot, crème fraîche, and pancetta. Toss in the slightly cooled potatoes and adjust seasoning with salt and pepper. Garnish with parsley.

SERVES: 2 as a side dish, 4 as a tapa
PREP TIME: 5 minutes
COOKING TIME: 20 minutes

YA YA CHERIE'S QUICK and DIRTY JAMBALAYA

I'm not claimin' it's strictly authentic, y'all—but if you want a tasty bowl of rice and goodness, give this a whirl.

2 tablespoons butter

2 tablespoons grapeseed oil

1 onion, chopped

1 green bell pepper, chopped

2 ribs celery, chopped

3 green onions, chopped

3 cubes frozen crushed garlic

1 jalapeño, chopped

1 teaspoon red chile pepper flakes, crushed

¼ teaspoon dried thyme

1 (12.8-ounce) package Trader Joe's Smoked Andouille Chicken Sausage, sliced ½-inch thick

2 cups chicken broth

½ cup white wine

1 (15-ounce) can chopped tomatoes in juice

3 cups long grain white rice

1 pound raw medium shrimp, peeled

1 cup Trader Joe's Just Chicken (optional)

GLUTEN-FREE

In a large sauté pan, melt the butter and oil over medium-high heat until sizzling. Add the "holy trinity" (the onion, bell pepper, and celery) and sauté until fragrant, about 3 minutes. Add the green onions, garlic, and jalapeño, and sauté 3 minutes. Add the crushed red chile pepper flakes and thyme and sauté until vegetables are tender, about 5 to 7 more minutes. Add the sliced sausage, chicken broth, wine, and tomatoes, and bring to a boil. Stir in the rice and bring back to the boil. Reduce the heat to low, cover, and simmer for 20 minutes. Remove the lid, stir the rice, and add the shrimp. (If using Just Chicken, add it now.) Cover the pan, remove from heat, and let stand 10 minutes. Uncover and check shrimp—if they are cooked through, the dish is finished. If not, tuck them into the rice and cover the pan for 5 more minutes.

SERVES: 6
PREP TIME: 15 minutes
COOKING TIME: 45 minutes

RED, WHITE, and BLUE FIRECRACKER POTATO SALAD

Perfect for Bastille Day, Fourth of July, or any summer celebration calling for red, white, and blue (or bleu)!

1 pound Trader Joe's Potato Medley, or a mixture of red, white, and blue (purple) boiling potatoes, cut into 1-inch cubes
½ cup crème fraîche
¼ cup Trader Joe's Organic Kansas City Style BBQ Sauce
4 green onions, chopped
½ red onion, chopped
salt and pepper

VEGETARIAN, GLUTEN-FREE

Bring a large pot of lightly salted water to a boil. Add the potatoes and cook until a skewer penetrates easily but the potatoes retain a slight firmness. Drain. Combine the crème fraîche and barbecue sauce. Add the sauce to the warm potatoes and toss to combine. Add the chopped green and red onions, toss again, and season to taste with salt and pepper. Serve at room temperature or chilled.

SERVES: 4
PREP TIME: 10 minutes
COOKING TIME: 15 minutes

KALE and FARRO TIMES 1,000

I love the bags of quick-cooking farro. Now that I live far from a Trader Joe's, I like to keep at least 5 bags on hand, in case one day I find it's been discontinued. The rustic, nutty grain reminds me of travels in Italy, and it's great to use in grain bowls or soups, or chilled in salads. This recipe is among my favorite ways to use it. It's basically just farro and kale, but it tastes like so much more!

3 tablespoons olive oil, divided
1 red onion, chopped
4 cubes frozen garlic
½ bag organic washed and chopped kale
1½ cups chicken or vegetable stock
1 (8.5-ounce) bag Trader Joe's 10 Minute Farro, cooked according to package directions
salt and pepper

VEGETARIAN (IF VEGETABLE BROTH IS USED)

In a large sauté pan, heat 2 tablespoons of oil and sauté the onion until it starts to soften, about 5 minutes. Add the garlic and sauté until fragrant, about 1 minute. Add the kale and sauté until wilted, 1 to 2 minutes. Add the stock and bring to a boil. Reduce heat and simmer until the kale is tender, about 12 minutes. Remove to a serving bowl. Heat the remaining olive oil and sauté the cooked farro to warm it and crisp it a little bit. Toss it with the kale and season to taste with salt and pepper.

SERVES 4 to 6
PREP TIME: 5 minutes
COOK TIME: 20 minutes

My favorite way to eat this is in a bowl with a jammy-yolked soft-cooked egg on top. Try stirring some Zhoug sauce through it, or some Trader Joe's Chili Onion Crunch.

SUMMER FARRO SALAD with CHERRY TOMATOES and FETA

This is one of those dishes that's equally good hot, room temperature, or chilled. The nuttiness of the farro combines really well with the brightness of the corn salsa and the salty, creamy feta.

1 (8.5-ounce) bag Trader Joe's 10 Minute Farro, cooked according to package directions

1 cup cherry tomatoes, halved

1 cup Corn and Chile Tomato-less Salsa

½ cup Trader Joe's Danish Feta cubes or crumbled feta

2 tablespoons olive oil

2 teaspoons red wine vinegar

chopped basil or mint, for garnish

salt and pepper

VEGETARIAN

In a large bowl, toss the cooked farro with the tomatoes, corn salsa, and feta. Add the olive oil and vinegar and toss to combine. Adjust the seasoning to taste with salt and pepper and garnish with basil or mint.

SERVES 4 to 6
PREP TIME: 5 minutes
COOK TIME: 10 minutes

If I'm going to serve this chilled, I'll leave the tomatoes out until I'm ready to serve it, as I think the flavor of tomatoes is brighter if not refrigerated.

Chapter 5

POULTRY

When time is tight, chicken or turkey is what's for dinner, chez moi. It's fast and easy on the wallet, and cooking is a virtual no-brainer. What more could you ask from the poultry case? You can take that poultry in so many flavor directions—it's the meat equivalent of tofu. Gussied up with curry sauce, barbecue sauce, pesto, or salsa, it's all good.

Even if I'm pressed for time, I generally reach for bone-in chicken pieces because they yield so much more flavor than their boneless, skinless counterparts. Keeping the meat on the bone also helps keep the meat from drying out. (If you doubt that there's a big difference in flavor, just think of the ingredients in a good pot of chicken broth—it's 90 percent bones, a few veggies, and water, and yet you get such a rich, chicken-y flavor after some simmering. It's the bones, baby!)

But boneless poultry also has its place in my kitchen. Slap a package of turkey cutlets in my cart and I can have a plate of Turkey with Green Chile Sauce on the table in the time it takes to cook the rice to go with it. And chicken thighs, even boneless, pack a flavor wallop. Sauté or stir-fry them with a couple handfuls of shredded carrots and baby squashes from the fresh produce section or with a bagful of frozen vegetables in sauce, and dinner doesn't get much quicker.

One of the things I really appreciate about Trader Joe's is that each section of the store is relatively small compared to a conventional grocery store, and especially compared to the big box stores. What that means to me is that they are constantly replenishing the shelves and refrigerated cases. This frequent turnover ensures a fresher product in the poultry case, and that means more delicious and healthful dishes on your table.

Kosher, free-range, or organic poultry—Trader Joe's has them all, and at far better prices than some of the fancy-schmancy grocery emporia. So grab a package of white or dark meat, or a whole roaster, and get ready to have a terrific TJ's meal.

TURKEY with GREEN CHILE SAUCE

Creamy, spicy goodness takes turkey to a new level. This is one of my favorite recipes from recent TJ's cooking classes. Serve with roasted butternut squash and brown rice for a warming autumn dinner.

1 pound turkey cutlets

1 tablespoon olive oil

3 cubes frozen crushed garlic

1 cup Blackthorn Fermented Cider or dry white wine

2 tablespoons Trader Joe's Hatch Valley Fire-Roasted Diced Green Chiles

½ cup ripe Brie, rind removed

salt and pepper

GLUTEN-FREE

Season the turkey cutlets with salt and pepper. In a medium sauté pan, heat the olive oil and sauté the garlic over medium heat for 2 to 3 minutes, until fragrant. Add the turkey cutlets in a single layer and cook until barely seared on both sides, about 2 minutes. (Work in batches, if necessary.) Remove to a platter.

Add the hard cider or wine to the pan and bring to a boil. Reduce heat and simmer until the cider is reduced by half, about 5 minutes. Return the cutlets to the pan and cook through. Remove again to the serving platter and keep warm. Add the chopped chiles and Brie to the sauté pan and simmer until the cheese melts and the sauce is thickened. Pour the sauce over the cutlets and serve.

SERVES: 4
PREP TIME: 5 minutes
COOKING TIME: 15 minutes

GENERAL TSAO CHICKEN WRAPS

Kids love to put these together, and they are as healthful as they are tangy-crunchy-good.

1 tablespoon grapeseed or canola oil
½ pound boneless chicken (thighs, breasts, or a combination), coarsely chopped
about ¼ cup Trader Ming's General Tsao Stir Fry Sauce
½ (10-ounce) bag shredded carrots
1 head large, sturdy lettuce, like romaine

In a medium sauté pan, heat the oil and sauté the chicken over medium-high heat until cooked through. (The time will depend on how small the chicken pieces are.) With a knife or in a food processor, chop the cooked chicken finely. Stir in the General Tsao sauce until the mixture is moist but not too drippy. Add the shredded carrots and bundle into lettuce leaves.

SERVES: 4
PREP TIME: 5 minutes
COOKING TIME: less than 10 minutes

HOT TODDY CHICKEN

Good for what ails ya!

2 pounds chicken thighs
2 teaspoons olive oil
1 tube Trader Joe's chicken Savory Broth concentrate
½ cup water
½ cup orange marmalade
2 tablespoons whiskey
1 tablespoon honey
pinch of red chile pepper flakes
salt and pepper

GLUTEN-FREE

Season the chicken thighs with salt and pepper. Heat the oil in a large sauté pan over medium-high heat and brown the chicken on both sides, in batches. When all of the chicken is browned, return it to the pan and pour in the concentrated chicken broth and water. Cover and simmer over low heat (10 minutes for boneless thighs, 25 for bone-in). Combine the marmalade, whiskey, honey, and red chile pepper flakes and pour into the pan, stirring to combine with the pan liquid. Simmer until the sauce is thickened and thighs are well-coated and cooked through.

SERVES: 4 to 6
PREP TIME: 15 minutes
COOKING TIME: less than 45 minutes

PESTO CHICKEN SALAD

While not a traditional Italian dish, this chicken salad has the flavors of a Ligurian summer day. Sip a glass of Pinot Grigio and dream of the Mediterranean.

¼ cup Trader Giotto's Pesto alla Genovese (in the refrigerated case)

3 tablespoons red wine vinegar

2 tablespoons olive oil

1½ cups Trader Joe's Just Chicken (or cooked chicken), coarsely chopped

1 (7-ounce) bag arugula or mixed baby greens

¼ English cucumber, chopped

½ cup shredded carrots

½ red onion, chopped

¼ cup toasted pine nuts

salt and pepper

GLUTEN-FREE

Whisk together the pesto, vinegar, and olive oil. Season to taste with salt and pepper. Toss the chicken with half the pesto mixture. In a large bowl, combine the arugula (or mixed greens), chopped cucumber, carrots, and red onion, and dress with the remaining pesto mixture. Adjust the seasoning to taste. Arrange the vegetables on a platter and top with the chicken. Sprinkle pine nuts over the salad.

SERVES: 2 to 4
PREP TIME: 10 minutes
COOKING TIME: none

MAPLE MUSTARD CHICKEN

A great pantry meal, this takes just moments to make and then hangs out in the oven while you pull the rest of the meal together. A quick salad and maybe some Trader Joe's Harvest Grains Blend, and you are good to go!

½ cup Dijon mustard

¼ cup maple syrup

1 tablespoon rice vinegar

1½ pounds boneless chicken thighs

salt and pepper

Preheat the oven to 450°F. Combine the mustard, maple syrup, and rice vinegar. Place the chicken in a single layer in an ovenproof casserole, and season with salt and pepper. Pour the mustard-maple syrup mixture over the chicken, turning to coat. Roast until the interior of the chicken thighs reach 155°F on a meat thermometer, about 20 minutes. Let the chicken rest for 5 minutes before serving.

SERVES: 4 to 6
PREP TIME: 5 minutes
COOKING TIME: 20 minutes

PROSCIUTTO TURKEY TENDERLOIN
with FINGERLINGS

This one is a keeper—a quick zap in the microwave gets the vegetables going quickly, then they finish roasting along with the turkey for a savory finale.

1 (1-pound) package fingerling potatoes, halved (or 1 pound boiling potatoes, cut in quarters)

1 (12-ounce) package fresh Trader Joe's Butternut Squash Zig-Zags

1 to 2 tablespoons olive oil

2 cubes frozen crushed garlic

3 tablespoons maple syrup

sprinkle of red chile pepper flakes

2 turkey tenderloins (or pork tenderloins)

4 ounces sliced prosciutto

GLUTEN-FREE

Preheat the oven to 425°F. Combine the potatoes and Butternut Squash Zig-Zags in an ovenproof and microwaveable casserole and drizzle with olive oil. Microwave for 4 minutes.

Combine the garlic, maple syrup, and a sprinkle of red chile pepper flakes. Reserve about 1 tablespoon of this mixture and rub the rest on the turkey (or pork) tenderloins.

Wrap the tenderloin in prosciutto. Place in the casserole on top of the potatoes. Roast 25 minutes. Drizzle with the remaining maple syrup mixture and roast until the internal temperature of the tenderloins is 150°F on a meat thermometer, 5 to 10 minutes. Let the tenderloin rest for 5 to 10 minutes before carving.

SERVES: 4 to 6
PREP TIME: 10 minutes
COOKING TIME: 30 minutes

Microwaving the vegetables speeds up the prep, but if you prefer, you can roast the potatoes and Butternut Squash Zig-Zags in the oven for about 20 minutes before adding the turkey.

  The I ♥ TRADER JOE'S® COOKBOOK

CHAMPAGNE CHICKEN with CHAMPIGNONS

Simple enough for a weeknight, elegant enough for company, this chicken dish is rich and flavorful. Serve over rice or pasta, with haricots verts (French green beans) or roasted asparagus.

1 tablespoon butter

1½ pounds boneless chicken breasts or thighs

2 cubes frozen crushed garlic

2 shallots, thinly sliced

6 ounces mushrooms, thinly sliced

¾ cup Champagne or sparkling wine

½ to ¾ cup heavy cream

salt and white pepper

GLUTEN-FREE

In a large sauté pan, heat the butter over medium heat and sauté the chicken until it loses its pink color, about 4 minutes on each side. Add the garlic and shallots to the pan, and sauté until the shallots are softened, about 4 minutes. Add the mushrooms and Champagne (it will fizz up, then subside) and season lightly with salt and white pepper. Cover the pan and simmer 10 to 15 minutes or until chicken is cooked through. Turn the chicken once halfway through the cooking time. Remove the chicken to a warm platter. Increase heat to high and reduce cooking liquid until about ¼ cup remains. Add the cream and reduce by half, about 4 minutes. Pour the sauce over the chicken on the platter and serve.

SERVES: 4
PREP TIME: 10 minutes
COOKING TIME: 30 minutes

SPICY-SWEET APRICOT-GLOSSED CHICKEN BREASTS

I love the pairing of the super garlicky spread with chicken (thank you Zankou Chicken!) and adding some zingy spice makes it even more alluring. I like equal parts of the garlic spread and either Italian Bomba Hot Pepper Sauce or Chili Onion Crunch as a sandwich spread or as a dip for veggies.

4 bone-in chicken breasts
1 tablespoon grapeseed oil
¼ cup Trader Joe's Organic Apricot Preserves
2 tablespoons Trader Joe's Garlic Spread-Dip
1 tablespoon Trader Joe's Italian Bomba Hot Pepper Sauce or Chili Onion Crunch
salt and pepper

Preheat the oven to 375°F. Season the chicken with salt and pepper and brown in a medium ovenproof sauté pan. Place the pan in the oven for 15 minutes. Mix together the jam, garlic spread, and Bomba and spread over chicken. Bake for another 10 to 15 minutes, until the chicken is cooked to 160°F and juices run clear. Let sit for 5 minutes before serving.

SERVES: 4
PREP TIME: 10 minutes
COOKING TIME: 45 minutes

Serve with farro or rice with some chopped dried apricots and pistachios. This glaze is good on pork as well.

Chapter 6

BEEF AND LAMB

"Beef. It's what's for dinner." Remember that ad campaign? There are plenty of times when it's still true. Whether you're a confirmed beefaholic or cutting back on the red stuff, if you partake at all, Trader Joe's has a small but mighty selection of cuts to delight your palate and your pocket. Some of the beef is grass-fed, some is Black Angus, and all of it is fresh and ready to grill, broil, or braise when you need to "get your beef on." From down-home tri-tip steaks and roasts, both great for barbecuing, to upscale cuts like New York strips and filet mignon, there's something to delight any carnivore. My favorite cut? It's gotta be a rib-eye—the butcher's cut—full of great beef flavor.

I'm somewhat of a purist when it comes to steaks—I don't eat them often, but when I decide to partake, I really want to taste the flavor of the meat itself. So generally, I'll salt and pepper the meat (or give it a Trader Joe's 21 Seasoning Salute!) and grill it on the rare side. If I'm feeling particularly luxe, I'll slice a pat of compound butter on the sizzling meat. Maybe Maître d'Hotel butter or Port and Gorgonzola butter—there are so many flavor combinations that are great with beef. If I'm feeling both luxe and lazy, a handful of crumbled Gorgonzola or Maytag blue cheese scattered on the steak as soon as it leaves the grill makes a decadent instant sauce. This is not to say I'm anti-marinade. There are several marinated cuts in the Trader Joe's meat case that I rely on for quick and yummy meals. Carne Asada Auténtica and Chicken Shawarma are a couple great quick-starts for meals.

BOOL, KOGI BEEF on COCONUT RICE with MACADAMIA NUTS and BASIL

Macadamia nuts lend a great crunch, and the mango and basil make the dish "pop" on the platter.

1 cup light coconut milk

1 cup water (or vegetable or chicken broth)

1 cup uncooked Trader Joe's Jasmine Rice from Thailand or basmati rice (or use frozen or precooked rice and omit water or broth)

salt

¼ cup macadamia nuts, chopped

handful of fresh basil leaves, chiffonaded

1 to 1½ pounds Trader Joe's Bool Kogi

½ fresh mango, sliced, or ½ package presliced mango, for garnish

In a medium saucepan, bring the coconut milk and water (or broth) to a boil. Stir in the rice and bring the liquid back to a boil. Reduce the heat to very low, cover, and cook with the lid on for 15 minutes. Remove from the heat, leaving the lid on, and let stand for 5 minutes. Remove the lid, fluff the rice, and season with a little salt. Stir in the chopped nuts. Just before serving, sprinkle with the basil. Grill or broil the bool kogi for 3 to 5 minutes per side. Serve the grilled or broiled beef strips on top of the rice, garnished with mango slices.

SERVES: 4 to 6
PREP TIME: 10 minutes
COOKING TIME: 25 minutes

If you love the flavor of coconut, increase the amount of coconut milk to 1½ cups and add ½ cup of water (in place of the 1 cup water or stock) to make the rice.

TRI-TIP ASADA with HEIRLOOM TOMATOES

As gorgeous as it is delicious, this dish puts a summer evening on the calendar any time of year.

1 Trader Joe's Carne Asada Auténtica tri-tip steak (about 1½ pounds)

4 large or 8 small heirloom tomatoes

1 ripe avocado

½ red onion

¼ to ½ cup Trader Ming's Sesame Soy Vinaigrette

Heat a grill to high heat and sear the tri-tip on both sides. Reduce the heat to medium and cover the grill. Cook until rare, or until the internal heat registers 130°F on a meat thermometer. (If cooking on a charcoal grill, mound the coals on one side and, after the tri-tip is seared, move it to the area without coals. Cover the grill so the meat will cook over indirect heat.) Let the meat rest at least 10 minutes before slicing it thinly. Slice the tomatoes and arrange on a platter. Slice the avocado and red onion and arrange along the edges of the platter. Dress lightly with the vinaigrette and arrange the sliced tri-tip in the center.

SERVES: 4 to 6
PREP TIME: 10 minutes
COOKING TIME: less than 30 minutes

SIRLOIN SALAD with A LATIN KICK

This can be on the table in about 10 minutes, and it sure beats the other type of "fast food"!

1 (5-ounce) bag of Trader Joe's Baby Spring Mix (or other lettuce mix)

1 tablespoon olive oil

¾ pound sirloin, thinly sliced

1 tablespoon balsamic vinegar

about ½ cup Trader Joe's Corn and Chile Tomato-Less Salsa

1 ripe avocado, sliced

salt and pepper

GLUTEN-FREE

Arrange the lettuce on a platter. Heat the olive oil in a large sauté pan and sauté the sirloin over medium-high heat until rare. Add the balsamic vinegar and heat through. Season to taste with salt and pepper and place on top of the greens. Spoon some of the corn salsa over the salad and top with avocado slices.

SERVES: 4
PREP TIME: 5 minutes
COOKING TIME: 10 minutes

PEPPERED BEEF and RICE MEDLEY

Texture, color, and crunch all come together in this recipe in a yummy jumble of rice and tender beef strips. A treat for the eyes and the taste buds.

¾ to 1 pound tender beef steaks (boneless rib-eye, tenderloin, or other cut), sliced into strips

1 tablespoon olive oil

coarsely ground black pepper

¼ (30-ounce) box frozen Trader Joe's Rice Medley

1 cup baby spinach leaves

½ cup shredded carrots

¼ English cucumber, cut into thin strips

1 tablespoon red wine vinegar

1 tablespoon soy sauce

2 tablespoons sesame oil

2 green onions, chopped

Bring a kettle of water to a boil for the vegetables. Brush the steak strips with the olive oil and sprinkle with the pepper. Heat a sauté pan and sauté the steak strips over medium-high heat for 2 to 3 minutes, until cooked but rare. Remove to a warm platter.

Cook the rice medley according to the package directions. Place the spinach leaves and shredded carrots in the bottom of a colander. When the water boils, pour it over the vegetables in the colander. The hot water will wilt the raw vegetables slightly. Toss the rice with the vegetables, cucumber, red wine vinegar, soy sauce, and sesame oil. Add the beef and garnish with the green onions.

SERVES: 4
PREP TIME: 10 minutes
COOKING TIME: 15 minutes

THAI BEEF SALAD

Improvise with other vegetables. Multicolored bell pepper strips, blanched snow peas, or mushrooms are all delicious and pretty in this salad as well.

1½ to 2 pounds flank steak
1 cup fresh lime juice, divided
½ cup soy sauce, divided
2 ripe tomatoes, cut in eighths
1 English cucumber, thinly sliced
1 red onion, thinly sliced
1 cup shredded carrots
1 jalapeño, minced
1 tablespoon brown sugar
1 cup fresh basil or mint leaves

Marinate the flank steak in ½ cup lime juice and ¼ cup soy sauce for 4 hours or overnight.

Toss the tomatoes, cucumber, onion, and carrots in a medium bowl with the remaining lime juice, soy sauce, jalapeño, and sugar. Remove the steak from the marinade, pat dry, and discard the marinade. Grill the steak over hot coals, broil, or sauté over high heat for 3 to 5 minutes per side. Let stand for 5 to 10 minutes, then slice thinly across the grain. Combine the beef and vegetables, tossing well. Add the basil or mint leaves, toss again, and serve.

SERVES: 4 to 6
PREP TIME: 15 minutes, plus marinating time
COOKING TIME: 10 minutes

BURGUNDY LAMB and CIPOLLINI

Don't be afraid of lamb. This is a great way to try this flavorful meat—the marinade is delicious and complements the luscious lamb flavor beautifully.

1 tablespoon olive oil

1 pound Trader Joe's Burgundy Pepper Lamb Tips

1 (8-ounce) bag peeled cipollini onions, cut in half

2 cubes frozen crushed garlic

½ cup red wine

½ cup beef broth

GLUTEN-FREE

In a medium sauté pan, heat the olive oil and sauté the lamb cubes over medium-high heat until browned on all sides. Add the onions and sauté for 2 minutes. Add the garlic and sauté until fragrant. Add the red wine, bring to a boil, reduce heat, and simmer for 2 to 3 minutes. Add the beef broth and simmer for 8 to 10 minutes, until the lamb and onions are tender and the sauce is reduced.

SERVES: 4
PREP TIME: 5 minutes
COOKING TIME: 20 minutes

Chapter 7

PORK

Chops, tenderloins, bacon, speck, pancetta, or prosciutto—I'll just confess up front to being a card-carrying, certified, die-hard porkaholic. When I'm recipe-testing and the dish lacks something, my first thought is what kind of pork to add. A stroll along the Trader Joe's meat aisle will generally offer up several great answers to that question.

If time is tight, I generally reach for pork tenderloins. They're super-affordable, there's no waste, they cook up fast, and there are thousands of ways to change up the flavor. With a simple basting of Trader Joe's Organic Kansas City Style BBQ Sauce or a maple syrup–mustard glaze, I can turn sliced pork tenderloin into a palate-pleasing dish my family will love. The loin chops go just as quickly from pan to platter with the help of a simple pan sauce or glaze.

While I love pork tenderloins, I hereby proclaim my belief that bacon is a miracle food. The smell of bacon cooking has tempted many a vegetarian off the path. My fondest hope is that bacon, like dark chocolate and red wine, will be declared good for us! While I'm not holding my breath on that one, I do indulge occasionally. After all, one ounce of bacon fat contains less saturated fat and cholesterol than butter, and packs a ton of flavor. I liberally interpret that to mean that bacon fat is nearly a health food!

So, if meat is on the menu at my house, it's very likely to be the "other white meat," although I personally prefer mine on the pink side. Pork is bred to be so lean these days, it's a shame to overcook it. A very slight blush is a pretty thing, especially when it comes to pork.

FRAT BRATS

I created this sandwich for my son Kevin when he turned 21. His fraternity brothers come to the cooking school hungry, and these hearty sandwiches can feed a bunch of them in a hurry.

1 (12-ounce) package Trader Joe's Uncured Bavarian Bratwurst

2 red onions, thinly sliced

1 (12-ounce) beer (We used MacTarnahan's Oregon Honey Beer, but you can use whatever you like.)

4 focaccia or panini rolls

about ½ cup Trader Joe's Corn and Chile Tomato-Less Salsa

Garnishes: sliced avocado, sliced Muenster or Havarti cheese, and sliced tomatoes

Place the bratwurst and sliced onions in a medium sauté pan and pour the beer over them. Bring the beer to a boil and simmer the bratwurst for 5 minutes. Turn the sausages over and continue to cook until the beer is nearly evaporated and the onions begin to soften and deepen in color, about 10 minutes. Remove the onions and set aside.

Cook the bratwurst until lightly browned on one side, then turn it to brown lightly on the other side. Remove it from the pan and cool slightly. Cut the sausages in half lengthwise. (If they are not cooked enough for your liking, return them to the pan, cut side down, for a few minutes to cook them more thoroughly.)

Split the focaccia rolls (like hamburger buns) and arrange a bratwurst on the bottom of each roll. Place some of the onions on top of each, and add a dollop of corn salsa. Garnish as desired with avocado, cheese, and tomatoes.

SERVES: 4
PREP TIME: 5 minutes
COOKING TIME: less than 20 minutes

MAPLE BALSAMIC PORK CHOPS

I'm a big fan of Grade B maple syrup. It's darker in color and, to my palate, deeper in flavor. And it's cheaper than the fancy-schmancy Grade A.

1 tablespoon grapeseed oil

4 Trader Joe's Butcher Shop Natural Boneless Pork Loin Chops

6 tablespoons maple syrup

2 tablespoons balsamic vinegar

1 tablespoon Dijon mustard

Preheat the oven to 375°F. In a medium sauté pan, heat the oil and brown the pork chops on both sides over medium-high heat (about 4 minutes per side.) Combine the maple syrup, balsamic vinegar, and mustard, and pour over the chops. Place in the oven and bake for 15 minutes, or until the pork is cooked through and light pink in color.

SERVES: 4
PREP TIME: 5 minutes
COOKING TIME: 25 minutes

MARSALA-ROASTED PORK

Here's another main dish that's great for entertaining. The sauce will make you want to lick the plate, so be sure to have something to soak up the delicious liquid.

½ (.88-ounce) package Trader Joe's Mixed Wild Dried Mushroom Medley (You'll find these near the pasta.)

1 (¾ to 1 pound) pork tenderloin

2 teaspoons olive oil

½ cup heavy cream

2 tablespoons Marsala

1 tablespoon Dijon mustard

salt and pepper

Preheat the oven to 400°F. In a coffee grinder or food processor, chop the dried mushrooms until they are pulverized. Season the mushroom powder with salt and pepper. Roll the tenderloin in the mushroom powder to coat it evenly. In a sauté pan large enough to hold the tenderloin, heat the olive oil and brown the meat on all sides. Remove the tenderloin to an ovenproof casserole. Combine the cream, Marsala, and mustard, and pour over the tenderloin. Roast until cooked through, about 15 minutes. Let the meat rest at least 5 minutes before slicing.

SERVES: 3 to 4
PREP TIME: 10 minutes
COOKING TIME: 20 minutes

ASIAN-FLAVORED PORK

Quicker than Chinese take-out! If you have leftover cooked rice, or if you use the TJ's frozen rice, this recipe flies together. The scoring of the meat accomplishes two objectives—it creates more surface area for the flavorful spice rub, and it looks so pretty.

4 thin pork loin chops

1 tablespoon salt

1 teaspoon ground cumin

1 teaspoon ground cinnamon

1 teaspoon minced fresh ginger

2 cubes frozen crushed garlic

2 teaspoons olive oil or grapeseed oil

4 cups cooked white rice

¼ to ½ cup Trader Ming's General Tsao Stir Fry Sauce or Trader Joe's Sweet Chili Sauce

Score the pork chops on both sides, in a diagonal pattern, about ⅛ inch deep. Combine the salt, cumin, cinnamon, crushed ginger, and garlic, and rub on both sides of the pork chops. In a medium sauté pan, heat the oil and sear the pork chops over medium heat on one side, about 3 minutes. Turn and cook on the other side, about 3 minutes. Serve over cooked rice with a splash of General Tsao sauce or Sweet Chili Sauce.

SERVES: 4
PREP TIME: 10 minutes
COOKING TIME: 10 minutes

CHERRY PORK with a KICK

Hands down, one of our favorites from the cooking school. Fast and packed with flavor.

1 pound pork tenderloin, cut into ¾-inch-thick medallions (rounds)

1 tablespoon olive oil

¾ cup Trader Joe's Cherry Preserves

3 tablespoons crème fraîche

dash of Trader Joe's Chili Pepper Sauce or Jalapeño Pepper Hot Sauce

salt and pepper

GLUTEN-FREE

Season the pork with salt and pepper. In a medium sauté pan, heat the oil over medium-high heat and sauté the pork medallions, in batches, until they are browned and nearly cooked through, about 6 minutes. Remove to a warm platter. In the same sauté pan, melt the cherry preserves and stir in the crème fraîche. Season to taste with hot sauce, salt, and pepper. Return the pork and any accumulated juices to the pan and simmer briefly to marry the flavors.

SERVES: 4
PREP TIME: 5 minutes
COOKING TIME: 15 minutes

PORK with CIDER

This dish is so great when the weather turns cool. Add some thick slices of apple or pear if you have some handy. It smells amazing as it simmers!

1 tablespoon olive oil

1½ pounds pork tenderloin, cut in bite-sized pieces

1 red onion, cut in eighths

½ teaspoon dried thyme, or leaves from 2 sprigs fresh thyme

1 cup Blackthorn Fermented Cider

1 tablespoon balsamic vinegar

salt and pepper

In a large sauté pan, heat the oil and sauté the pork and onion wedges over medium-high heat until browned. Add the thyme, hard cider, and balsamic vinegar, and bring to a boil. Reduce the heat, season lightly with salt and pepper, and simmer until the pork is cooked and the cider is thickened, about 8 minutes. Adjust seasoning to taste.

SERVES: 4
PREP TIME: 5 minutes
COOKING TIME: 15 minutes

Serve something starchy with this, like mashed potatoes or rice, so you can sop up all the sauce!

PORK and PEPPERS

A weeknight favorite, this goes together quickly and uses only ¼ cup of wine. You know what to do with the rest …

2 tablespoons olive oil
1 small onion, sliced thinly
2 cubes frozen crushed garlic
5 to 6 sweet mini peppers, sliced
1 (¾- to 1-pound) pork tenderloin, cut into ½-inch-thick medallions (rounds)
¼ cup Sauvignon Blanc or other dry white wine
1 tablespoon fresh oregano, chopped, or 1 teaspoon dried oregano
salt and pepper

GLUTEN-FREE

In a large sauté pan, heat the olive oil and sauté the onion for 3 to 4 minutes over medium-high heat. Add the garlic and peppers and sauté for about 5 minutes more, until peppers are tender. Season the pork lightly with salt and pepper. Add the pork to the sauté pan and cook until browned on all sides, about 5 minutes. Add the wine (and the dried oregano, if using) and simmer for about 3 to 4 minutes, until the wine is slightly reduced. If using fresh oregano, add at this point. Adjust seasonings to taste with salt and pepper.

SERVES: 4
PREP TIME: 15 minutes
COOKING TIME: 20 minutes

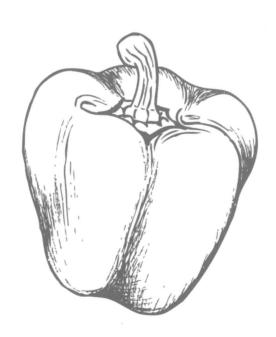

SPANISH-STYLE PORK

This dish is great on the center of the plate or as a small-plate, tapa-style dish.

1 (¾- to 1-pound) pork tenderloin, cut into ½-inch-thick medallions (rounds)

2 tablespoons olive oil, divided

2 cubes frozen crushed garlic

2 cups sliced mushrooms

½ cup dry sherry

¾ cup orange juice, divided

½ cup sliced green olives stuffed with pimientos (optional)

salt and pepper

GLUTEN-FREE

Season the pork medallions with salt and pepper. Heat 1 tablespoon of oil in a medium sauté pan. Brown the pork over medium-high heat on both sides and set aside. Add the rest of the olive oil and sauté the garlic until fragrant, 2 to 3 minutes. Add the mushrooms and sauté until they release their moisture and it evaporates, about 5 minutes. Remove to a platter.

Combine the sherry with ½ cup of the orange juice and pour the liquids into the sauté pan. Bring to a boil, reduce heat, and simmer for about 3 minutes. Return the pork to the pan and simmer for 2 to 4 minutes, or until it is cooked through. Remove the pork to a serving platter.

Add the remaining orange juice and simmer until the sauce thickens slightly, about 2 minutes. Stir the sliced olives into the mushrooms and put the mixture on the pork. Pour the sauce on top and serve.

SERVES: 4
PREP TIME: 10 minutes
COOKING TIME: 20 minutes

MARGARITA PORK CHOPS

The flavor just pops on these babies ... plus, you can use some of the leftover ingredients for some liquid libation!

1 teaspoon ground cumin

4 Trader Joe's Butcher Shop Bone-In Frenched Center-Cut Pork Chops

1 tablespoon olive oil

3 cubes frozen crushed garlic

¼ cup chicken broth

½ cup tequila

2 tablespoons fresh lime juice

4 tablespoons butter

½ jalapeño, minced

salt and freshly ground black pepper

Combine the cumin with 2 teaspoons of salt and about ½ teaspoon of freshly ground pepper. Season the pork chops well on both sides with this mixture. (You may have some seasoning mix left over.) In a large sauté pan, heat the oil and brown the chops well, 4 to 5 minutes per side, over medium-high heat. Remove the chops to a warmed platter.

In the same sauté pan, sauté the garlic until fragrant, 1 to 2 minutes. In a separate bowl, combine the chicken broth, tequila, and lime juice. Remove the pan from the heat, add the liquid, and return to the heat. (Have a lid ready to cover the pan in case the alcohol ignites—by combining the liquids, the alcohol has been diluted, but it may flare up). Bring the liquid mixture to a boil and reduce to about ¼ cup. Add the butter and any juices that have accumulated on the platter. Swirl the pan until the butter is incorporated. Season to taste with the minced jalapeño, salt, and pepper. Pour the sauce over the chops.

SERVES: 4
PREP TIME: 10 minutes
COOKING TIME: 20 minutes

ROASTED PORK LOIN with FIG SAUCE

This recipe is perfect for cooler evenings. The parsnips and figs pair really well with the pork, and the house smells fabulous as the dish roasts.

2 to 2½-pound boneless pork loin roast, at room temperature

1 tablespoon olive oil

½ cup red wine

½ jar Trader Joe's Fig Butter

2 tablespoons Trader Joe's Honey Pale Ale Mustard

1 package parsnips, peeled and sliced about ½ inch thick

1 red onion, sliced

8 dried figs, halved

salt, pepper, and Trader Joe's Multipurpose Umami Seasoning Blend

Preheat the oven to 350°F. Season the pork roast with salt and Umami Seasoning Blend. In a medium ovenproof sauté pan, heat the olive oil and brown the pork on all sides. Remove the pork to a cutting board.

Add the red wine to the pan, bring to a boil, reduce the heat, and simmer for 2 minutes. Pour the wine into a bowl and stir in the Fig Butter and mustard. Arrange the sliced parsnips and red onion on the bottom of the pan and scatter the halved figs over them. Pour about ¼ of the Fig Butter mixture over the vegetables. Place the browned pork on top of the vegetables and roast 25 minutes.

Pour the remaining red wine/Fig Butter mixture over the pork and roast until internal temperature of pork is 140°, about 30 minutes. Let rest for 5 minutes before slicing. Adjust seasoning with salt, pepper, and Umami Seasoning Blend. Serve with roasted vegetables and pan juices.

SERVES: 4 to 6
PREP TIME: 15 minutes
COOKING TIME: about an hour

The Fig Butter is seasonal, so stock up! It's amazing on a grilled cheese sandwich, on a cheese or charcuterie platter, or in a vinaigrette. The Umami Seasoning Blend is fabulous and hoardable. Great on roasted meat or vegetables, in soups, on rice, or on pasta.

Chapter 8

SEAFOOD

I'm really picky about where I buy my fresh fish. Generally, I prefer to buy it from a real, live fishmonger who has kept it on a bed of crushed ice. This helps me assess the freshness of the fish, because one whiff will tell the tale if the fillets are less than fresh. While that's not possible at Trader Joe's, I'm willing to bend my rule there for one simple reason: turnover. The fresh fish case is quite small in most TJ's stores, and it's constantly being restocked, so nothing sits there for long. While it is tough to give the fish the sniff test through the plastic wrap, by being vigilant about the packing date, I've had very good luck with the fresh fish purchased at my Joe's. The prices are quite fair, especially when we're talkin' sashimi-grade ahi or wild salmon. The price discount can be big enough that you can pick out a nice bottle of Sauvignon Blanc with your savings. Forget coupons, that's the kind of wallet relief I appreciate!

The frozen fish case at Trader Joe's is replete with choices. Most of the fish there were caught in the wild, not farmed. There has been finger-pointing on both sides of the wild fish vs. farmed fish fray, and while I generally opt for wild fish, I believe the nutritional benefits of fish in your diet are important enough that, for me, farmed fish is better than no fish. In some parts of this country, that's still the only option. The prices are great (duh … it's TJ's), and the variety varies by season. One of my favorite things to stash in my fridge is the Wild Argentinian Red Shrimp. These are meaty morsels with great flavor, and they sauté up in minutes. They're absolutely on my hoarding list because the supply is limited and seasonal. Watch the frozen case for these and stock up for wonderful flavor in shrimp cocktails, stir-fry dishes, or shrimp salads.

I'd love to see some wild-caught U.S. shrimp in that frozen case. I'd even pay a bit more for it, in order to support our fishermen and women who've been hit hard by hurricanes and oil spills. I bet a lot of other folks would, too!

CASHEW-CILANTRO SHRIMP

Barely cooked, the herby sauce maintains uber-fresh flavors in this super-quick dinner dish.

½ cup cashews

3 tablespoons grapeseed oil, divided

1 (0.75-ounce) package cilantro, stems trimmed but not completely removed

3 cloves garlic (or 3 cubes frozen garlic)

1 jalapeño, stem removed

juice of ½ lime

1 tablespoons soy sauce

2 teaspoons brown sugar

1 pound raw shrimp, defrosted, shelled, and deveined

salt and pepper

In a food processor, chop the cashews coarsely. Add 2 tablespoons of the grapeseed oil and the cilantro and pulse to combine. Add the garlic and jalapeño and chop. Add the lime juice, soy sauce, and brown sugar and whirl to combine. Season with salt and pepper. Set aside.

In a medium sauté pan, heat the remaining 1 tablespoon of grapeseed oil and sauté the shrimp until just pink. Add the cashew-cilantro sauce and toss to combine. Adjust the seasoning to taste with salt, pepper, and additional lime juice.

SERVES: 4
PREP TIME: 5 minutes
COOKING TIME: 10 minutes

Serve this over rice, or even better, the super-delish TJ's Scallion Pancakes from the frozen veg section.

SHRIMP on POLENTA PILLOWS

Superfast and deeply delicious, this dish makes a great first course, or toss together a green salad to go with it and call it dinner!

1 (18-ounce) roll Trader Joe's Organic Polenta (precooked), sliced into ½-inch rounds

olive oil for brushing or olive oil spray

1 (8.5-ounce) jar Trader Joe's Julienned Sun-Dried Tomatoes, with about 2 tablespoons of the oil removed (see note)

3 cubes frozen crushed garlic

2 tablespoons capers

½ cup dry white wine

1 pound frozen raw large shrimp, thawed and peeled

Preheat the broiler. Brush or spray the polenta rounds with olive oil and place on a baking sheet. Broil, watching carefully, until browned, about 5 minutes.

In a medium sauté pan, drizzle 1 tablespoon of the oil from the jar of sun-dried tomatoes and sauté the garlic over medium-high heat until fragrant, about 2 minutes. Add the contents of the jar (sun-dried tomatoes and remaining oil), capers, and white wine. Sauté until the sun-dried tomatoes are softened and heated through. Add the shrimp and sauté until cooked through and coated with sauce, about 5 minutes. Serve over the polenta rounds.

SERVES: 4 to 6
PREP TIME: 5 minutes
COOKING TIME: 15 minutes

Use the 2 tablespoons of reserved oil from the jar of sun-dried tomatoes to scramble with eggs or brush on crostini. It's full of flavor from the tomatoes and herbs.

GRILLED SWORDFISH with MANGO SALSA

This salsa is great with grilled chicken or pork as well—or just chips!

MANGO SALSA:

1 cup chopped fresh mango

1 jalapeño, seeded and minced

¼ cup chopped red onion

¼ cup chopped fresh cilantro

juice of 1 lime, or more as needed

salt and freshly ground black pepper

pinch of cayenne pepper

SWORDFISH:

1½ pounds frozen swordfish or any firm-fleshed fish, defrosted

2 teaspoons grapeseed oil

GLUTEN-FREE

FOR THE MANGO SALSA: Combine the mango, jalapeño, onion, cilantro, and lime juice in a medium bowl. Let stand at least 30 minutes to meld the flavors. Adjust the seasoning as needed with salt, pepper, and more lime juice. Use a pinch of cayenne if you want more heat than the jalapeño provides.

FOR THE SWORDFISH: Season the fish with a little salt and pepper. In a medium sauté pan or skillet, heat the grapeseed oil over medium-high heat. Cook the fish until a knife blade inserted into the center comes out warm to the touch, 2 to 3 minutes per side. Serve with the salsa.

SERVES: 4 to 6

PREP TIME: 10 minutes, plus marinating time

COOKING TIME: 10 minutes

SHRIMP in HARD CIDER

Hard cider is delicious, and having a well-deserved revival in the United States. It's often served as a tasty alternative to beer, which I really appreciate, since I'm not a big beer fan. The dry, slightly effervescent tang of pear or apple cider brings a crispness to this quick dinner dish.

1 pound raw large shrimp, peeled and deveined

1 tablespoon butter

2 cloves garlic, minced

¼ cup Calvados (or other brandy)

1 cup hard cider (Blackthorn Fermented Cider or Ace pear cider)

salt and pepper

Remove the tail shells from the shrimp, if they are attached. Pat the shrimp dry. In a large sauté pan, heat the butter and sauté the garlic over medium-high heat until fragrant. Add the shrimp and sauté just until pink, 2 to 3 minutes. Remove the shrimp to a platter and carefully add the Calvados (or brandy) to the pan. If it does not ignite, either tip the pan toward the flame (taking care not to spill any of the liquor) or light with a match to burn off the alcohol. Add the cider and bring to a boil. Reduce the heat and simmer until liquid is reduced by about half. Return the shrimp to the pan, toss to warm and coat with sauce, and season to taste with salt and pepper.

SERVES: 4
PREP TIME: 5 minutes
COOKING TIME: 10 minutes

GAMBAS y JAMBON

A great addition to a tapas spread. The flavors of shrimp and pork complement each other so well, and the spiciness from the hot sauce sneaks up on you!

1 pound raw large shrimp, peeled and deveined (reserve shells, if you peeled them yourself)

1 tablespoon olive oil

1 tablespoon butter

5 cubes frozen crushed garlic

¼ cup chopped Serrano ham, pancetta, or prosciutto

Trader Joe's Chili Pepper Sauce or Jalapeño Pepper Hot Sauce, to taste

salt and pepper

GLUTEN-FREE

In a sauté pan large enough to hold the shrimp in a single layer, heat the olive oil and butter to bubbling over medium-high heat. If you have the shrimp shells, sauté them until they turn pink and the oil-butter mixture is perfumed with the aroma of shrimp. Remove the shells with tongs or a slotted spoon, shaking the liquid back into the pan. (If no shells are available, begin here.) Add the garlic and sauté until it is fragrant, 2 to 3 minutes. Add the ham, pancetta, or prosciutto and sauté 2 minutes. Add the shrimp and sauté just until pink and opaque, 2 to 4 minutes. Season with salt, pepper, and hot sauce. Serve on baguette toasts as an appetizer or over rice for a main dish.

SERVES: 4 as an appetizer, 2 to 3 as a main course
PREP TIME: 10 minutes
COOKING TIME: 15 minutes

MARGARITA SHRIMP

The margarita theme is a recurring one in these pages—hey, I grew up in Southern California, and margaritas are a summer staple there!

1 tablespoon grapeseed oil

1 medium yellow onion, chopped

3 cubes frozen crushed garlic

1 pound raw large shrimp, peeled and deveined

¼ cup tequila

2 ripe tomatoes, chopped

½ cup shredded carrots

juice of 2 limes

1 ripe avocado, diced

salt and pepper

In a medium sauté pan, heat the oil and sauté the onion over medium-high heat until it begins to soften, 3 to 4 minutes. Add the garlic and sauté until fragrant, 1 to 2 minutes. Add the shrimp and sauté for 3 to 4 minutes. Carefully add the tequila, away from the heat. (Or flambé it if you want some drama, but have a lid nearby to quell the flame, if necessary). Add the tomatoes and carrots and sauté 2 minutes. Add the lime juice and cook another minute, or until shrimp is just cooked through. Add the diced avocado, toss to warm through, and season to taste with salt and pepper.

SERVES: 4 as an appetizer, 2 to 3 as a main course
PREP TIME: 10 minutes
COOKING TIME: 15 minutes

GLAMOUR SALMON

I hate to think of how long ago I saw a version of this recipe in Glamour magazine. Let's just say I was a new bride—and it was in another century. I was so proud of myself when I served this to guests at a dinner party because it was elegant and tasty. That hasn't changed over the ensuing decades.

1 to 1½ pounds salmon fillets
⅓ cup honey
2 tablespoons soy sauce
juice of 1 lemon
1 tablespoon sesame oil
¼ teaspoon red chile pepper flakes
salt and pepper, to taste

Place the fillets in a resealable plastic bag. Combine the remaining ingredients and pour over fish. Preheat the broiler and broiler pan while the fish marinates, about 20 minutes. Place the fillets, skin-side down, on a broiler pan, and place in the oven at least 4 inches from the heating element. Broil 5 to 7 minutes, until nearly opaque.

SERVES: 4 to 6
PREP TIME: 25 minutes (mostly marinating time)
COOKING TIME: less than 10 minutes

SOUTH OF FRANCE HALIBUT

When I imagine lazy summer days in Arles or Avignon, I don't envision hours of prep work for delicious meals. This dish goes together in the time it takes to sip one glass of rosé.

1 (9.5-ounce) jar Trader Joe's Olive Tapenade
2 cubes frozen crushed garlic
½ cup dry white wine
1 pound wild halibut, frozen or defrosted
salt, pepper, and red chile pepper flakes

In a medium sauté pan, combine the tapenade, garlic, and white wine and bring to a simmer. Add the fish and simmer until it is cooked through (about 6 minutes for thawed fish, and about 20 minutes for frozen). Season to taste with salt, pepper, and red chile pepper flakes.

SERVES: 4
PREP TIME: 5 minutes
COOKING TIME: less than 10 minutes for thawed fish, and about 20 minutes for frozen

Chapter 9

PASTA

Honestly, who isn't immediately comforted by a softly steamy, fragrant, cheese-stringed, yielding bowl of pasta? A day has to be nearly disastrous before the thought of that very meal won't lift my spirits. The pasta aisle may be my favorite one at Trader Joe's, and pasta is definitely my favorite dinner for a harried night. I think most of us turn to pasta when hunger is high and time or energy is in short supply. Pasta is a great way to tart up leftovers so no one will recognize (and thereby complain about) them.

If I am so distracted or overtired that thinking about what to cook is overwhelming, I find that if I get the pasta water going and salted and just let myself sway around the kitchen, pasta-making ingredients will almost magically bring themselves to my fingertips, like the brooms in *The Sorcerer's Apprentice*. Last night was one of those nights. (Hey! cookbook writing is hard!) So I poured a glass of Sauvignon Blanc, got the salted water boiling, grabbed a bag of farfalle, and tossed some in. I had a shallot, so I chopped that up, then poured a glug of good TJ's olive oil in a sauté pan. Once the shallot smelled great, I noticed that I had a hank of asparagus hanging around, so I whacked the spears into pieces and threw them in to relax. There was a handful of mushrooms, so in it went, and by then the pasta was nearly tender. I sloshed about a cupful of pasta water into a cup for later and drained off the rest. A glug of cream and a knob of goat cheese went into the pan of vegetables and immediately surrendered into creamy sauce. I literally ripped the remaining meat off a rotisserie chicken from the fridge and tossed the chunks in to warm up. I squeezed the contents of a tube of chicken broth concentrate on top and splashed in the pasta water I'd saved. A quick stir, and I dumped the cooked noodles into the pan. A couple grinds of black pepper from the great TJ's plastic pepper grinder, and dinner had practically cooked itself. All I did was stroll around my kitchen with a glass of wine for 15 minutes (and create this bonus recipe for you!).

Pasta shapes are so varied, and the different varieties are fun to pair with so many flavor profiles. The sharp flavors of olives and lemons, the peppery notes of arugula or radicchio, the smooth creaminess of mascarpone or crème fraîche, the crunch of nuts or toasted bread crumbs. Any of these combine beautifully (and quickly) with Trader Joe's pastas for a fast, satisfying carb-lover's bowlful of love. A gigantic pot of well-salted water is the key. "Salty like the sea," I always recall my culinary school instructor bellowing. You want enough water for that pasta to be able to swish around like clothes in the washing machine. Too little water makes for stuck-together clumps of noodles. Use the package instructions as a guide on timing, but trust yourself more than those—fish out a strand when it looks pliable and take a nibble. The texture should be the slightest bit firm at the center, but sans crunch. The pasta will continue to cook a little bit as you drain it and as it rests in the strainer, so you want a little resistance to the tooth before you do that. But no crunch—"al dente" means "to the tooth," not "break a tooth"!

We all need to let our inner carb fiend out to play every now and again. Gluten-free, whole wheat, or traditional, fresh or dried, Joe's has a pasta that will have you setting a pot of water to boil and reaching for the colander. (Oh, and opening the wine. Don't forget that important step!) Many of these dishes are a meal in a bowl on their own, but pairing them with a great salad is never a bad idea.

The I ♥ TRADER JOE'S® COOKBOOK

OLIVE BUTTERFLIES

I love to serve this in summer as an accompaniment to grilled meat or fish. The tapenade delivers a tangy saltiness, and the goat cheese melts into a lightly creamy sauce.

1 (16-ounce) bag farfalle

1 (10-ounce) jar green Trader Joe's Olive Tapenade (or Roasted Red Pepper and Artichoke Tapenade)

4 ounces goat cheese (Trader Joe's Chèvre, Silver Goat Chèvre, or Madame Chèvre)

handful of cherry tomatoes, halved (optional)

salt and pepper

VEGETARIAN

Cook the pasta in boiling, salted water until tender. Drain and return to the saucepan with the tapenade and goat cheese, stirring to incorporate and melt the cheese. Stir in tomatoes, if using. Adjust seasoning to taste with salt and pepper.

SERVES: 4
PREP TIME: 5 minutes, if using halved tomatoes
COOKING TIME: 10 minutes

We sometimes call these bowties, but the Italians call them farfalle, which means butterflies. Much more poetic than bowties, don't ya think? This is great hot, served at room temperature, or chilled.

PASTA MOLLICA

Mollica means crumb in Italian, but in this dish, it also means delicious! Students at the cooking school always looked skeptical before they tasted the deeply nutty, crunchy flavor these little nuggets bring to the pasta. It's an old technique: When times were tough, people learned to use up everything and to substitute the browned crumbs of leftover bread for more expensive nuts or even for cheese. In the current economy, mollica may become a household term again.

4 tablespoons butter or olive oil, divided

2 cubes frozen crushed garlic

½ cup fresh bread crumbs (don't use dry bread crumbs from the package for this)

1 (16-ounce) bag long pasta (such as linguine or spaghetti), cooked al dente and drained

salt and pepper

VEGETARIAN, VEGAN (IF OLIVE OIL AND VEGAN BREAD ARE USED)

Melt 2 tablespoons of the butter in a medium sauté pan (or use 2 tablespoons of oil) and sauté the garlic over medium heat for 1 to 2 minutes, or just until fragrant. Add the bread crumbs and sauté until browned and crispy, about 5 minutes. (The crumbs should be very nicely colored and crisp, but be careful not to burn them.) Toss the cooked pasta with the reserved butter or olive oil, and then with the bread crumbs. Season to taste with salt and pepper.

SERVES: 4
PREP TIME: 5 minutes
COOKING TIME: 10 minutes

To make fresh bread crumbs, finely chop some good bread in a food processor. I like to use the Trader Joe's Organic Whole Grain Loaf for this, but a good baguette will work well, too.

FARFALLE with GREEN BEANS and FETA

I love the flirty look of farfalle. The green beans add nutrition to this dish, of course, but they also look so pretty, and the crumbled feta gets sprinkled in like confetti.

1 (16-ounce) bag farfalle

1 cup fresh green beans, cut into 3-inch pieces or 1 cup fresh haricots verts (French green beans) or frozen French green beans, whole

3 ounces feta cheese

salt and pepper

½ pound cooked medium shrimp (optional)

1 tablespoon butter (optional)

VEGETARIAN (IF MADE WITHOUT SHRIMP)

Bring a large pot of salted water to a boil. Add the pasta and cook until nearly al dente. (The pasta should be cooked about three-quarters of the way through.) Add the green beans and continue to cook until the beans are tender, 3 to 5 minutes. Drain the pasta and beans and place in a serving dish. Toss in the feta, crumbling as you add it, and stir to combine. Taste the pasta before you season it because the feta is salty—you may only need some freshly ground black pepper.

SERVES: 4
PREP TIME: 5 minutes
COOKING TIME: 15 minutes

Adding ½ pound of cooked large shrimp to this makes it a meal in a bowl. Just sauté the shrimp for 2 to 3 minutes in 1 tablespoon of butter over medium-high heat to warm through, and then toss with the pasta.

LEMON-VODKA PASTA

These simple but classic flavor combinations never disappoint. I guess that's why they're classics! This goes really well with roasted chicken or fish.

1 (16-ounce) bag long, thin pasta (linguini, spaghetti, or capellini)

1 (8-ounce) container mascarpone

zest and juice of 1 lemon

2 tablespoons vodka (or limoncello)

½ cup fresh basil leaves, chiffonaded

salt and pepper

VEGETARIAN

Bring a large pot of salted water to a boil. Cook the pasta al dente. While the pasta cooks, in a medium saucepan, warm the mascarpone with the lemon juice and vodka. Season to taste with salt and pepper. When the pasta is cooked, drain it and toss it with the fresh basil and lemon zest. Add the pasta to the sauce in the pan and toss to coat. Adjust seasonings to taste with salt and pepper and serve.

SERVES: 4
PREP TIME: 5 minutes
COOKING TIME: 10 minutes

When you need the zest and juice of a lemon, always zest first and juice second. It's so much easier to get the zest off of the intact lemon instead of trying to zest the two halves.

PASTA with PUMPKIN SAUCE

The Trader Joe's canned pumpkin is organic and is really great quality. I don't even want to tell you how many cans of it I squirrel away when it arrives in the stores. Since it's a seasonal item, I need to make sure I have enough to last the year.

1 (16-ounce) bag pasta (see note)

1 cup Trader Joe's canned Organic Pumpkin

1 cup chicken broth

splash of Trader Joe's Chili Pepper Sauce or Jalapeño Pepper Hot Sauce, or sprinkling of red chile pepper flakes

salt and pepper

½ cup toasted walnuts, coarsely chopped

2 teaspoons fresh sage, finely minced

shaved Parmesan cheese (optional)

VEGETARIAN (IF VEGETABLE BROTH IS USED)

Bring a large pot of salted water to a boil. Cook the pasta al dente. Reserve about a cup of the cooking water before draining the pasta and placing it in a large bowl. In a small saucepan, combine the pumpkin purée and chicken broth and bring to a simmer. Pour over the cooked pasta, adding the reserved cooking liquid, ¼ cup at a time, until the sauce reaches the desired consistency. Toss to combine and season to taste with a little hot sauce or red chile pepper flakes, salt, and pepper. Add the chopped walnuts and minced sage and toss again. Garnish with shaved Parmesan, if using.

SERVES: 4
PREP TIME: 5 minutes
COOKING TIME: 15 minutes

Long or short shapes of pasta work equally well in this dish, so use whatever you have on hand.

PASTA PROVENÇAL

Serving this for lunch is the quickest route to an imaginary afternoon in Avignon. Pair it with a glass of rosé and you may never want to come back home.

1 (16-ounce) bag linguine or another long pasta shape
½ cup shredded carrots
1 tablespoon Trader Joe's Capers in Vinegar, rinsed
½ cup pitted, mixed olives, coarsely chopped
1 (6-ounce) can Trader Joe's Skipjack Tuna in Water (or another high-quality tuna)
1 tablespoon olive oil
salt and pepper

Bring a large pot of salted water to a boil. Cook the pasta al dente. Place the carrots in a strainer and pour the pasta in to drain. (The boiling water will blanch the carrots perfectly.) Place the pasta and carrots in a large serving bowl and toss with the capers, chopped olives, and tuna. Dress to taste with olive oil, salt, and pepper.

SERVES: 4
PREP TIME: 5 minutes
COOKING TIME: 10 minutes

You can substitute half a jar of Green Olive Tapenade for the chopped olives, if you are in a hurry.

GORGONZOLA FUSILLI

It just sounds wonderful, doesn't it? Gor-gon-zola Fu-si-lli ... almost like an Italian mantra. With the optional addition of pancetta or bacon, I just might make it my own mantra!

1 (16-ounce) bag fusilli
2 tablespoons butter
1 shallot, minced
1 leek, thinly sliced
2 tablespoons heavy cream
3 ounces Trader Joe's Crumbled Gorgonzola Cheese
freshly ground black pepper
about 3 ounces diced pancetta or cooked and crumbled Niman Ranch Applewood Smoked Dry-Cured Bacon (optional)

VEGETARIAN (IF NO PANCETTA OR BACON IS USED)

Bring a large pot of salted water to a boil. Cook the pasta al dente and reserve about a cup of the cooking water before draining the pasta and setting it aside. In the same pot, melt the butter, then sauté the shallot and leek slices over medium heat until slightly caramelized, about 5 minutes. Add the cream, warm through, and add the crumbled Gorgonzola. Allow the cheese to soften. Add the cooked pasta back into the pot and toss to combine. If a more liquid consistency is desired, add a little of the reserved pasta water. Season with freshly ground black pepper. Toss in the pancetta or cooked bacon, if using.

SERVES: 4
PREP TIME: 5 minutes
COOKING TIME: 15 minutes

A MEAL on ITS OWN PASTA

The Southern Greens Blend couldn't be better for you. The goat cheese adds a creamy element, and it's so subtle in this dish, even people who aren't fans of goat cheese will gobble this up.

1 (16-ounce) bag fusilli or farfalle

6 strips bacon, snipped or chopped

2 shallots, thinly sliced

1 tablespoon olive oil

½ bag (about 3 cups) Trader Joe's Southern Greens Blend, coarsely chopped

2 cubes frozen crushed garlic

4 ounces soft goat cheese (Trader Joe's Chèvre, Silver Goat Chèvre, or Madame Chèvre)

salt and freshly ground black pepper

Bring a large pot of salted water to a boil. Cook the pasta al dente. Reserve about a cup of the cooking water before draining the pasta and setting it aside. Once the pasta is drained, in the same pot, cook the bacon until the fat is rendered and the bacon is about half-cooked. Add the shallots and sauté over medium heat until tender and fragrant, 2 to 3 minutes. Add the olive oil and the greens. Sauté until the greens wilt. If it seems too dry, add a few tablespoons of the reserved pasta water. Add the garlic and sauté until it is aromatic, 1 to 2 minutes. In a large bowl, add the greens mixture to the pasta and toss to combine. In the same pot, heat the goat cheese with ½ cup pasta water until it is creamy, then toss with the pasta. Use the remaining pasta water if you want a saucier consistency. Season to taste with freshly ground black pepper and a little salt, if needed.

SERVES: 4
PREP TIME: 10 minutes
COOKING TIME: 20 minutes

The bacon and goat cheese will add saltiness, so taste before you add salt.

LOTSA LEMON PASTA

I like to think that the healthy arugula balances out the crème fraîche … Whatever—a little bit of this tasty pasta is all I need to feel satisfied.

1 (7-ounce) bag arugula

1 (7.5-ounce) container crème fraîche

juice and zest of 2 lemons, divided

1 cup grated Parmesan cheese, divided

1 (16-ounce) bag fusilli (or other small pasta)

freshly ground black pepper

VEGETARIAN

Roughly chop the arugula and place in a colander. In a large bowl, stir together the crème fraîche, lemon juice, half the lemon zest, and half the Parmesan cheese. Bring a large pot of salted water to a boil and cook the pasta al dente. Drain the pasta into the colander with the arugula. (The hot water will wilt the arugula slightly.) In the large bowl, toss the pasta with the crème fraîche sauce and season to taste with freshly ground black pepper. Garnish with the remaining grated cheese and lemon zest.

SERVES: 4 to 6
PREP TIME: 10 minutes
COOKING TIME: 15 minutes

RED WINE PASTA

I first ate this at a crazy little trattoria in Florence, where they throw you out of the place if you order your steak well-done. While I would never do that, just to be safe, I stuck to the wine-y pasta and was so happy I did!

1 (16-ounce) bag spaghetti, capellini, or other long pasta

1 bottle red wine (an inexpensive but drinkable Zinfandel or Syrah)

4 cubes frozen crushed garlic

red chile pepper flakes

2 tablespoons butter

salt and pepper

½ (8-ounce) container Trader Joe's Crumbled Gorgonzola Cheese

½ cup toasted walnuts

VEGETARIAN

Bring a large pot of salted water to a boil and cook the pasta for about 3 minutes, until just pliable. Drain the pasta. In a large sauté pan, bring about three-quarters of the wine to a boil. Add the garlic cubes and a few shakes of red chile pepper flakes. When the garlic has dissolved, add the pasta and cook, stirring frequently, until pasta is al dente. Stir in the butter and season to taste with salt and pepper. Serve individual portions (or put the spaghetti on a platter) and garnish with crumbled Gorgonzola and toasted walnuts.

SERVES: 4
PREP TIME: 5 minutes
COOKING TIME: 20 minutes

FETTUCCINE with SHRIMP and SAFFRON CRÈME

Saffron is the most expensive spice on the planet because it is incredibly labor-intensive to harvest. But Trader Joe's carries an excellent-quality saffron in an adorable cork-topped jar for a great price.

1 (16-ounce) bag fettuccine

1 tablespoon olive oil

1 tablespoon butter

3 cubes frozen crushed garlic

generous pinch of Trader Joe's Spanish Saffron, crumbled

1 cup dry white wine

1 pound raw large shrimp, peeled and deveined (or ½ pound shrimp and ½ pound scallops)

½ cup crème fraîche

salt and pepper

pinch of red chile pepper flakes (optional)

zest of 1 lemon, for garnish

Cook the pasta in rapidly boiling salted water until al dente. Reserve about a cup of the cooking liquid before draining and setting aside. In a medium sauté pan, heat the olive oil and butter over medium heat. Add the garlic and saffron and sauté over medium heat until fragrant, about 2 minutes. Add the wine, bring to a boil, reduce the heat, and simmer until reduced, about 4 minutes. Add the shrimp and sauté until just cooked through, about 4 minutes. Stir in the crème fraîche and season to taste with salt, pepper, and red chile pepper flakes (if using). Toss with cooked pasta, adding some of the cooking liquid if desired for a saucier consistency. Garnish with lemon zest.

SERVES: 4
PREP TIME: 10 minutes
COOKING TIME· 15 minutes

As FAST as TAKE-OUT CHICKEN POBLANO RAVIOLI with MEXI-CORN and JALAPEÑO SAUCE

This one is super fast, but packed with zingy flavor. Throw together a salad or pick up a premade one from—well, you know where—and dinner's done!

1 (14-ounce) bag frozen Trader Joe's Mexican Style Roasted Corn

1 (8-ounce) package Creamy Chicken & Poblano Ravioli

2 tablespoons plain yogurt or crème fraîche

Trader Joe's Jalapeño Pepper Hot Sauce, to taste

Cook the Mexican corn and ravioli according to package directions. Combine in a bowl. Stir together the yogurt or crème fraîche and a few teaspoons of jalapeño sauce and adjust to desired level of heat. Drizzle over corn and ravioli and serve.

SERVES: 2
PREP TIME: 5 minutes
COOKING TIME: 15 minutes

There are several seasonal ravioli flavors. If you find one you love, stock up. They freeze well. Just pop them into boiling water frozen and add a few minutes to the cooking time.

BRUSSELS SPROUT RAVIOLI with CRUCIFEROUS CRUNCH

The Cruciferous Crunch veggie blend really does it for me—I use it with blue cheese dressing for a hearty salad, drop it by handfuls into stir-fries or soups, or toss it with some pasta, a little olive oil, and a sprinkle of Quattro Formaggio.

1 tablespoon olive oil

½ bag Trader Joe's Cruciferous Crunch

1 bulb fennel, thinly sliced

2 tablespoons butter

4 whole sage leaves

1 package Trader Joe's Brussels Sprouts & Caramelized Onion Ravioli, cooked according to package directions

Trader Giotto's Balsamic Glaze and shaved Parmesan, for garnish

salt and pepper

In a medium sauté pan, heat the olive oil over medium-high heat. Add the Cruciferous Crunch and sliced fennel, and sauté until just tender, 5 minutes. Add ½ cup water and stir until the vegetables are soft, another 5 minutes. Season with salt and pepper. Arrange on serving dish and keep warm.

In the same pan, melt the butter, add the sage leaves, and heat over medium-low heat until the butter is browned and nutty and the sage is aromatic. Toss the cooked ravioli in the sage butter and place atop the sautéed vegetables. Drizzle with balsamic glaze and scatter shaved Parmesan over the top.

SERVES: 2 to 3
PREP TIME: 5 minutes
COOKING TIME: 15 minutes

Use some of the ravioli cooking water for the liquid in the sauté. The little bit of starch in the water adds some body to the veggies.

The sage leaves can be used to garnish the dish, or left in the hot pan to crisp up a bit more. I love to munch on them—cook's treat!

Chapter 10

VEGETABLES

Whether fresh or frozen, the array of vegetables at Trader Joe's will get you eating your greens … and your oranges, reds, yellows, and browns. Isn't that what the dieticians say? "Eat the rainbow." TJ's makes it easy and tasty to follow that advice. The bags of cleaned and sliced mushrooms are so handy for quick sautés, pasta sauces, or salads, and the shredded carrots are a shortcut I take nearly every week. Sure, I know I'm paying more for the convenience factor, but they save me so much precious time that I'm willing to scrimp elsewhere. Also, my knife skills are decent, but it would take me eons to get all those perfect little slivers out of a bunch of whole carrots! I love to sneak those into a tomato sauce to balance out the acidity. Of course, they're great in a salad, or a wrap, or pasta … you'll find a ton of uses for those little slivers of sweet, colorful crunch.

The fresh vegetable area is full of ingredients that are prepped for your quick cooking pleasure, from the pre-trimmed French green beans called haricots verts to the cut-up cauliflower, to the pre-chopped mirepoix (for really crazy days). As for me, most days I actually enjoy the rhythm of my knife gliding through the carrots, onions, and celery as I get my vegetables ready for whatever's on tap. But at certain crunch times, knowing that the prepped vegetables are waiting can really mean the difference between home cooking and take-out. And I'm always in favor of home cooking, even if it means some corner-cutting.

For purists, Trader Joe's has shelves stocked with potatoes and onions of every hue, as well as a glorious palette of peppers. I especially love the Minisweet Bell Peppers. I call them the "weeknight pepper," because when time is tight, these little gems really come through. They have few, if any, seeds, and since that cottony membrane that's sometimes found in larger bell peppers isn't present in the little guys, chopping them takes mere seconds. I cut crosswise, starting at the tip and working toward the stem end, stopping just shy of the top, where a few little seeds may lurk. I enjoy the look of the little "Olympic rings" that result from this technique, but if a more minced texture is needed, it only takes a few seconds to run a knife through the circles of pepper to achieve a nicely chopped pile o' peppers. These sweet little beauties are also terrific cut in half lengthwise and used as a scoop for hummus or another tasty dip.

The vegetable freezer case is full of inspiration, too, whether it's the terrific French green beans or the roasted corn, complete with smoky charred flavor. The vegetable blends can perk up a dinner plate with great color, texture, and flavor. So whether fresh or frozen is your preference, Trader Joe's has a great selection of vegetables to get you eating what's good for you.

MIDDLE EASTERN BEETS

I love the look of this dish. It reminds me of the simple, flavorful dishes in the popular Ottolenghi cookbooks. Great as part of a mezze platter, or as a side dish.

4 beets (fresh or precooked in package), quartered

olive oil

4 tablespoons Trader Joe's Mixed Nut Butter

about 2 tablespoons Trader Joe's Garlic Spread-Dip

chopped pistachios

VEGETARIAN

Preheat oven to 400°F. Toss the beets in olive oil. Place them on a rimmed baking sheet and roast—25 to 30 minutes for fresh beets, 10 minutes for precooked (just to get a little roasted flavor and warm them). Spread the nut butter on a serving plate and place the beet quarters on top. Dollop with the garlic spread and garnish with chopped pistachios.

SERVES: 4
PREP TIME: 5 minutes
COOKING TIME: 10 to 30 minutes

I like to get a bit of roasted flavor on the beets if they've been precooked. This one is good warm, room temp, or cold. Drizzle with Trader Joe's Italian Bomba Hot Pepper Sauce or Chile Onion Crunch if you want to kick up the spice.

BABY ZUCCHINI with PESTO, PANKO, and PARM

Super simple—a perfect side dish for a busy night, when you want to feel just a little bit fancy.

1 bag baby zucchini

about ¼ cup Trader Giotto's Pesto alla Genovese

½ cup panko crumbs

½ cup grated Parmesan

VEGETARIAN

Preheat the oven to 400°F. Place the zucchini on a rimmed baking sheet and spoon pesto over it. Roll the zucchini to thoroughly coat in pesto. Combine the panko crumbs and Parmesan and sprinkle evenly over the zucchini. Roast until the zucchini is tender and crumbs are crunchy, about 15 minutes.

SERVES: 4
PREP TIME: 5 minutes
COOKING TIME: 15 minutes

TJ's carries several types of pesto. I prefer the refrigerated container, usually found near the salsas.

ROASTED ZUCCHINI and MUSHROOMS with PESTO

These smell amazing while they're roasting, and they look as good as they taste. Throw in some red onion, if there's some handy.

1 pound (about 4 medium) zucchini

1 (8-ounce) container crimini mushrooms

½ red onion, sliced (optional)

1 tablespoon olive oil

1 (7-ounce) container Trader Giotto's Genova Pesto (in the refrigerated section), divided

1 (4-ounce) container Trader Joe's Crumbled Goat Cheese

VEGETARIAN, GLUTEN-FREE

Preheat the oven to 425°F. Cut the zucchini into about 1-inch rounds. Toss the zucchini, mushrooms, and red onion (if using) with olive oil and arrange on a baking sheet. Roast until tender, 15 to 20 minutes. Remove the vegetables to a serving dish, toss with about half of the pesto, and sprinkle with crumbled goat cheese. Serve with the remaining pesto on the side.

SERVES: 4 to 6
PREP TIME: 5 minutes
COOKING TIME: 20 minutes

SUGAR SNAP PEAS, CORN, and BACON with BASIL BUTTER

The basil butter is also great on freshly roasted or steamed ears of corn, or even on a steak or pasta.

BASIL BUTTER:
½ cup firmly packed basil leaves
1 cube frozen crushed garlic
½ cup butter
zest of 1 lemon and juice of half
salt and pepper

SNAP PEAS, CORN, AND BACON:
4 strips bacon, chopped
1 (12-ounce) package fresh Trader Joe's Sugar Snap Peas
½ cup Trader Joe's Corn and Chile Tomato-Less Salsa

GLUTEN-FREE

FOR THE BASIL BUTTER: Place the basil leaves in a food processor and chop finely. Add the garlic cube and butter, and process to combine. Add the lemon juice and zest, and process again. Season to taste with salt and pepper. Wrap in parchment paper or plastic wrap and chill until ready to use.

FOR THE SNAP PEAS, CORN, AND BACON: In a medium sauté pan, cook the bacon until almost crisp. Add the sugar snap peas and sauté over medium-high heat for 3 to 4 minutes, until tender. Remove from the pan with a slotted spoon, leaving excess bacon drippings behind. In a serving bowl, toss the peas and bacon with the corn salsa. Top with a tablespoon or two of basil butter and stir to melt the butter. Refrigerate or freeze the rest for another use.

SERVES: 2 to 4
PREP TIME: 5 minutes
COOKING TIME: 10 minutes

GREEN BEANS with CAMBOZOLA SAUCE

This sauce is so rich and luscious, I could just drink it—but the green beans make this a much healthier idea.

1 package green beans, trimmed (or asparagus, or a combination of both)

4 tablespoons heavy cream or crème fraîche

6 ounces Cambozola or other soft blue cheese

salt and pepper

VEGETARIAN, POSSIBLY GLUTEN-FREE (CHECK CAMBOZOLA LABEL)

Cook the green beans in rapidly boiling, salted water until crisp-tender, 6 to 8 minutes. Drain and refresh in cold water. In a medium saucepan, heat the cream over low heat and melt the cheese. Add the green beans and toss to coat. Adjust seasonings to taste with salt and pepper.

SERVES: 4
PREP TIME: 5 minutes
COOKING TIME: 10 minutes

GREEN BEANS with RED ONION and CREAMY FETA DRESSING

This dish is great as is, or you can toss in some leftover steamed or roasted new potatoes for a heartier version.

1 (16-ounce) package fresh green beans, trimmed and steamed

½ red onion, thinly sliced

DRESSING:

½ cup plain yogurt

¾ cup feta cheese, crumbled

1 tablespoon lemon juice or red wine vinegar

freshly ground black pepper

2 tablespoons chopped basil, for garnish

VEGETARIAN

Arrange the green beans on a serving plate and scatter most of the red onion slices over the surface, reserving a few. Whisk together the dressing ingredients. (The dressing will be thick, with pieces of feta throughout.) Dollop the dressing over the salad and garnish with reserved red onion slices and basil.

SERVES: 4 to 6
PREP TIME: 10 minutes
COOKING TIME: 10 minutes

The frozen French green beans would work for this recipe, too—defrosted, of course!

ROASTED BUTTERNUT SQUASH with PECANS, DRIED CHERRIES, and BLUE CHEESE

The flavors in this dish could not be more autumnal (a word I truly love). The sage adds an earthy undertone, the colors mimic those of fallen leaves, and the blue cheese brings such depth of flavor. I could eat this all fall!

½ bag Trader Joe's Cut
Butternut Squash or 1 pound
butternut squash cubes

1 red onion, sliced

pinch of dried sage

about 1 tablespoon olive oil

½ cup chopped pecans

¼ cup dried cherries

¼ cup crumbled blue cheese

salt and pepper

VEGETARIAN, GLUTEN-FREE

Preheat the oven to 400°F. Arrange the squash cubes and sliced onions in a single layer on a rimmed baking sheet. Season with salt, pepper, and sage, and drizzle with olive oil. Roast for 15 minutes. Scatter the pecans over the top and roast for another 5 minutes. Remove the squash from the oven and toss with the dried cherries and blue cheese. Adjust seasonings to taste.

SERVES: 4
PREP TIME: 5 minutes
COOKING TIME: 20 minutes

MUSHROOM MARSALA SAUCE

This sauce is so deeply flavorful, you'll find a million ways to use it. I've served this with roasted pork, with pasta or polenta, or on top of greens as a warm winter salad.

¼ cup dried mushrooms (Trader Joe's Mixed Wild Dried Mushroom Medley)

2 tablespoons olive oil

2 tablespoons butter

4 shallots, minced

1 pound fresh mushrooms, sliced (see note)

3 ounces (half can) tomato paste

salt and pepper

½ cup Marsala

1 cup chicken or vegetable broth

VEGETARIAN (IF MADE WITH VEGETABLE BROTH), GLUTEN-FREE

Soak the dried mushrooms in enough hot water to cover until they are softened, about 20 minutes. Strain, reserving the soaking liquid. Coarsely chop the mushrooms and set aside.

Heat the oil and butter in a large skillet over medium heat, add the shallots, and sauté until tender, about 5 minutes. Add the reconstituted dried mushrooms and the fresh mushrooms to the shallots, and sauté until mushrooms are dry and softened, about 5 minutes. Add the tomato paste and sauté until the tomato paste coats the mushrooms and begins to glaze the bottom of the pan. Season lightly with salt and pepper.

Off the heat, add the Marsala, then return to the heat over a low flame and simmer until dry, 2 to 3 minutes. Add the reserved soaking liquid from the mushrooms and the chicken or vegetable stock. Bring to a boil, reduce heat, and simmer, covered, for about 10 minutes. Remove the lid and simmer for 10 more minutes. Season to taste with salt and pepper.

SERVES: 4 to 6
PREP TIME: 20 minutes
COOKING TIME: 40 minutes

Save some time by using the 1-pound bag of presliced mushrooms. They are already cleaned, which saves even more time.

MASHED SWEET POTATOES

My kids are not big sweet potato fans, but they devour these. You can substitute some goat cheese for the crème fraîche, too.

3 pounds sweet potatoes, peeled and cubed
¼ cup crème fraîche
2 tablespoons butter
2 cubes frozen crushed garlic
salt and pepper
dash of Trader Joe's Chili Pepper Sauce or Jalapeño Pepper Hot Sauce

VEGETARIAN, GLUTEN-FREE

Place the sweet potatoes in a medium saucepan and cover with water. Bring to a boil, reduce heat, and simmer until potatoes are tender, about 15 minutes. (Cooking time will depend on the size of the sweet potato cubes.) Drain the potatoes and return them to the pan. Add the crème fraîche, butter, and garlic, and stir until melted. Mash the potatoes into this mixture until smooth. Season to taste with salt, pepper, and hot pepper sauce.

SERVES: 4 to 6
PREP TIME: 10 minutes
COOKING TIME: 20 minutes

Thinned with a vegetable or chicken broth, this makes a great soup. Just add about a cup of broth after you mash the sweet potatoes, season to taste, and stir over medium heat until the mixture is smooth.

SCALLOPED CORN

An old-fashioned technique for corn, but there's nothing outdated about the taste.

2 tablespoons butter
1 shallot, thinly sliced
½ red bell pepper, chopped
3 cups fresh or frozen corn kernels
½ cup heavy cream
¼ teaspoon dried thyme or 1 teaspoon fresh thyme
salt and pepper
½ cup fresh bread crumbs
¼ cup grated Parmesan cheese

VEGETARIAN

Preheat the oven to 350°F. In a small sauté pan, melt the butter and sauté the shallot and red pepper over medium-high heat for about 4 minutes, or until softened. In a medium bowl, combine the sautéed pepper and shallot with the corn, cream, thyme, and some salt and pepper, to taste. Place in an ovenproof casserole. Combine the bread crumbs and Parmesan cheese and sprinkle over the top of the corn mixture. Bake for about 20 minutes, until bubbling and warmed through.

SERVES: 4
PREP TIME: 5 minutes
COOKING TIME: 25 minutes

ROASTED FENNEL, CRAYON CARROTS, and PARSNIPS with MAPLE GLAZE

Fall is my favorite time to roast all kinds of veg. Give me a sheet pan and just about any cruciferous or root vegetable, and some olive oil and I'm a happy eater. I love the autumn colors of this combo.

1 bulb fennel, sliced in ½-inch slices

3 Trader Joe's Organic Carrots of Many Colors, sliced in half, lengthwise and then halved lengthwise again

2 parsnips, cut the same way as the carrots

2 tablespoons olive oil, divided

1 tablespoon maple syrup

1 tablespoon Trader Joe's Honey Pale Ale Mustard

salt, smoked paprika, and pepper

VEGETARIAN

Preheat the oven to 425°F. Toss the prepared vegetables in 1 tablespoon of olive oil and season with salt and smoked paprika. Place in a single layer on a rimmed baking sheet and roast for 15 minutes, stirring once.

In a small bowl, whisk together the remaining tablespoon of olive oil, maple syrup, and mustard and drizzle over the vegetables. Return to the oven for 5 to 10 minutes, until the vegetables are tender and glazed. Adjust seasoning with more salt, if needed, and black pepper.

SERVES: 4
PREP TIME: 10 minutes
COOKING TIME: 25 minutes

If you like things a little spicy, use a tablespoon of Trader Joe's Chili Onion Crunch in place of the second tablespoon of olive oil in the glaze. Watch closely so the chile and onion crispy bits don't burn.

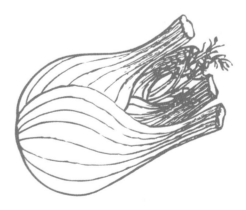

Chapter 11

DESSERTS

Dessert is back. For decades, the dessert course was forsaken in the United States—or eaten with a hearty helping of guilt or justification. But now, the thinking seems to be that depriving oneself makes the forbidden fruit more irresistible. As Julia Child used to advise—"Everything in moderation, including moderation." A little something sweet—I'm talking a two- or three-bite treat—can lift your spirits like nothing else. Or my spirits, anyway.

Most of the desserts in this chapter are based on fruit or contain dark chocolate, and we all know those are full of healthful antioxidants. So they're practically health food, right? While I may be stretching the point a wee bit, I do think that dessert, in moderation, is good for our emotional well-being. A little frippery can brighten an otherwise dull day, and who doesn't appreciate that?

With the new sweeteners on the shelves at Trader Joe's these days, you can play with substituting agave syrup or stevia for sugar and feel better about them than the processed sugar-bombs available in some places. Anything you make from these pages will have ingredients you can pronounce. Compare the ingredients in the amazing Trader Joe's frozen All Butter Puff Pastry with the puff pastry in the freezer section at other stores. They're like night and day—the TJ's ingredients are far superior, and it shows in the finished product. I don't even want to tell you how many boxes of this divine stuff I have in my freezer at any given moment. It's currently stocked seasonally, so hoard it like mad during the holidays, and use it all year.

If time is short, you can always skip these recipes and plunder the frozen-food case at Joe's for some great prepared goodies. My gymnast daughter used to devour the Trader Joe's Gone Bananas! chocolate-dipped frozen bananas by the boxful. I know a certain Joe who recommends eating the frozen carrot cake while it's still frozen—just grab a spoon and dig in!

RASPBERRY CARAMEL TURNOVERS

These are great do-aheads, and you can keep them in the fridge for a few days before baking or freeze them and bake a few at a time when you need a sweet treat.

1 package Trader Joe's All Butter Puff Pastry, defrosted but kept cold

1 (17.5-ounce) jar Trader Joe's Fresh Raspberry Preserves

5 caramels from a 10-ounce container Trader Joe's Dark Chocolate Covered Caramels, cut in half (you'll have a half left over for quality control!)

VEGETARIAN

Preheat the oven to 400°F. Roll the pastry out a bit, and cut into nine 3-inch squares. Spread the pastry with about a teaspoonful of raspberry preserves and place half a caramel in the center. Fold the pastry, corner to corner, to form a triangle, and press the edges with a fork to seal. Chill for 15 minutes in the freezer. Bake until the pastry is golden, 18 to 20 minutes. Cool slightly before eating—the filling is very hot!

SERVES: 9
PREP TIME: 15 minutes
COOKING TIME: 20 minutes

BERRY-ZIN SAUCE

I took cooking classes years ago from a wonderful cooking teacher, Hugh Carpenter. Hugh has written many great cookbooks and teaches classes in Napa, California. This is a variation on a dessert sauce from one of his classes that I've made for decades. The whole house will smell amazing as this simmers. It's great on ice cream, on pound cake, or as a finishing dessert sauce for cakes. In theory, it lasts at least a week in the refrigerator. In practice (at least at my house), it doesn't last nearly that long.

1 bottle Zinfandel (drinkable but not expensive)

1 (16-ounce) bag frozen Trader Joe's Fancy Berry Medley (or 12-ounce bag of frozen raspberries)

1 cup sugar

several grinds of black pepper

VEGAN, GLUTEN-FREE

Place all ingredients in a sauté pan (not a saucepan—you want more surface area for more efficient reduction) and bring to a boil. Reduce the heat and simmer for about 30 minutes, until the mixture is reduced to 2 cups. Strain through a sieve to remove seeds.

SERVES: 1½ cups
PREP TIME: 5 minutes
COOKING TIME: 30 minutes

SILKY, SINFUL CHOCOLATE TART

TJ's pie crust is amazing. I encourage students to leave the rolling pin out on the counter with little bits of dough clinging to it. Everyone will assume you made the crust yourself, and I see no reason to contradict that assumption!

1 Trader Joe's Gourmet Pie Crust (in the frozen-food section), defrosted (refreeze the remaining one for another use)

2 to 3 tablespoons Trader Joe's Fresh Raspberry Preserves (or another flavor)

8 ounces Trader Joe's Dark Chocolate, chopped

1¼ cups heavy cream

1 egg

2 egg yolks

3 tablespoons butter, at room temperature

1 pint fresh raspberries, for garnish (optional)

½ (7.5-ounce) container crème fraîche, softly whipped and slightly sweetened, for garnish (optional)

VEGETARIAN

Preheat the oven to 400°F. Roll the pie dough out a little and fit it into an 8- or 9-inch tart pan with a removable bottom. Cover with crinkled parchment, then add a layer of pie weights (or dried beans or uncooked rice). Bake 12 minutes, carefully remove the parchment along with weights (or beans or rice), and bake an additional 5 to 7 minutes, until the dough loses its wet appearance. Cool to room temperature. Spoon the preserves onto the crust and spread evenly.

Place the chopped chocolate in a heatproof bowl. In a small saucepan, heat the cream over low heat to a simmer, then pour the hot cream over the chocolate. Stir until the chocolate melts and combines evenly with the cream. In a separate bowl, stir together the whole egg and yolks, then add about half the warm chocolate and cream mixture, stirring. (This is called tempering, and it prevents the eggs from scrambling.) Add this mixture back into the chocolate and stir to combine well. Add the butter and stir to combine. Pour into the baked tart crust on top of the preserves and return to the oven for 18 minutes. The center of the tart will appear to be barely set, but it will firm up as it cools. Allow to cool at least 30 minutes before serving. Garnish with fresh raspberries and whipped crème fraîche, if desired. This tart is quite rich, so slice it thinly.

SERVES: 8
PREP TIME: 5 minutes
COOKING TIME: less than an hour, plus cooling time

Crème fraîche is perfect when you want something a little less sweet than whipped cream. Place the crème fraîche in a bowl; beat with a wire whisk until it billows with soft peaks. You can sweeten it, if you like, with a tablespoon or two of sugar or agave syrup.

GINGERBREAD with MASCARPONE and PEARS

The gingerbread mix is seasonal, so stock up, because as far as I'm concerned, it's always the right season for this treat!

1 (14-ounce) box Trader Joe's Gingerbread Cake Mix with Crystalized Ginger Pieces

butter or spray oil

1 egg

½ (8-ounce) container mascarpone

¼ cup sugar

1 cup ripe pears, chopped

VEGETARIAN

Preheat the oven to 350°F. Prepare the gingerbread mix according to package directions. Lightly butter or spray an 8-inch baking pan and spread half the gingerbread batter into the pan. Stir together the egg, mascarpone, sugar, and pears. Scatter dollops of the mascarpone mixture into the gingerbread batter. Cover with the remaining gingerbread batter. Bake until a skewer inserted into the gingerbread comes out clean, about 35 minutes. (If the skewer comes out with mascarpone on it, try a different spot.)

SERVES: 8
PREP TIME: 5 minutes
COOKING TIME: 35 minutes

For a charming variation, slice the pears and arrange them on the bottom of the cake pan in a spiral pattern. Spoon the gingerbread batter on top and bake. The pretty pear pattern will then be on top. Whisk together the mascarpone and sugar, then dollop the mixture on slices of the baked, unmolded cake.

BETTER-THAN-TIRAMISU

Such a quick and easy dessert to make when berries are gorgeous! Ladyfingers are "seasonal" at TJ's—what season IS ladyfinger season, I wonder? Apparently it's winter, so stock up so you'll be sure to have enough to last all year!

1 (10.5-ounce) jar Trader Joe's Lemon Curd

1½ (8-ounce) containers mascarpone

1 tablespoon frozen fruit juice (orange or another complementary flavor of your choice) defrosted but not diluted

2 tablespoons Grand Marnier or other citrus liqueur

1 package Trader Joe's Soft Lady Fingers

about 2 cups fresh berries (if using strawberries, hulled and sliced)

VEGETARIAN

With an electric mixer (or by hand), beat the lemon curd just enough to lighten the texture. Add the mascarpone and beat until combined, being careful not to overbeat. (The mascarpone can become grainy quickly if overbeaten, so be careful if using a mixer—just a few seconds will do the trick.) Set aside.

Combine the juice concentrate and Grand Marnier in a small bowl. Dip the flat side of each ladyfinger into the mixture and place half of them, dipped side up, in an 8 x 8-inch casserole dish. Spread half the lemon curd–mascarpone mixture over the ladyfingers and top with half the berries. Repeat the dipping and layering of ladyfingers, top with the remaining lemon curd–mascarpone mixture, then add the rest of the berries. Cover with plastic wrap and refrigerate at least 1 hour.

SERVES: 6
PREP TIME: 10 minutes
COOKING TIME: none

Don't use berries that aren't gorgeous. If peaches or nectarines are lovelier, use those, peeled and sliced.

TJ'S TRIFLE

This can be thrown together in just a few minutes, but the flavor is terrific.

1 package Trader Joe's Triple Ginger Snaps (or another favorite cookie)

1 cup heavy cream

2 tablespoons Chambord black raspberry liqueur

1 (8-ounce) container mascarpone

1 to 2 tablespoons sugar

2 cups strawberries, raspberries, blackberries, or blueberries, or a combination (sweetened to taste, if needed)

VEGETARIAN

Pulverize the cookies into crumbs using a food processor (or put them in a large double resealable plastic bag and crush them with a rolling pin) and set aside. Whip the cream to soft peaks, sweetening with sugar, as desired. Stir in the Chambord and then add the mascarpone, stirring to combine. In individual glasses or a large glass dish, layer some of the cream-mascarpone mixture, some berries, and some cookie crumbs. Repeat until you have three or four layers, ending with the cookie crumbs.

SERVES: 6
PREP TIME: 15 minutes
COOKING TIME: none

MINI VANILLA WAFER CHEESECAKES

This recipe is just waiting to be played around with. Pop some berries in before you bake them, or maybe a little piece of caramel. Crushed gingersnaps would be great as the base, too.

12 Trader Joe's Organic Vanilla Wafer Cookies

½ cup sugar

2 eggs

8 ounces cream cheese, at room temperature

8 ounces mascarpone, at room temperature

1 teaspoon vanilla

zest of 1 lemon

Trader Jacque's Fleur de Sel Caramel Sauce, for garnish

VEGETARIAN

Preheat the oven to 325°F. Place paper liners in a 12-hole muffin pan and place a vanilla wafer in the bottom of each. With an electric mixer, combine the sugar and eggs, then add the cream cheese, mascarpone, vanilla, and lemon zest, and mix to combine. Pour over the vanilla wafers, dividing evenly. Bake until set, 20 to 25 minutes. Cool before serving. Top each mini-cheesecake with a drizzle of caramel sauce.

SERVES: 12
PREP TIME: 10 minutes
COOKING TIME: 25 minutes

DOUBLE BLACKBERRY TART

The flavors of blackberries and almonds go so well together. A scoop of the terrific TJ's vanilla ice cream would put this over the top.

1 Trader Joe's Gourmet Pie Crust, defrosted (refreeze the remaining one for another use)

1½ cups blanched, slivered almonds

½ cup sugar

4 ounces butter

2 eggs

¼ teaspoon vanilla

1 tablespoon flour

¼ cup Trader Joe's Blackberry Preserves

1½ cups fresh blackberries

vanilla ice cream (optional)

VEGETARIAN

Preheat the oven to 375°F. Roll the pie dough, if needed to repair cracks, and press into a 9-inch tart tin or pie pan. Chill the crust while the filling is prepared. Place the almonds in a food processor and pulse to chop. Add the sugar and process until powdered. Add the butter and blend to combine. Add the eggs, vanilla, and flour and process again to combine.

Spread the preserves on the bottom of the unbaked pastry shell. Cover with the almond mixture, spreading carefully and evenly. Arrange the blackberries on top and bake the tart until it is set and fragrant, about 35 minutes. Serve and top with ice cream, if desired.

SERVES: 8
PREP TIME: 10 minutes
COOKING TIME: 35 minutes

ALMOND-PLUM GALETTE

This is great with a combination of pears and raspberries in place of the plums. Use whatever looks great in the fruit aisle.

⅔ cup blanched, slivered almonds

3 ounces butter

½ cup brown sugar

2 eggs

1 tablespoon flour

1 teaspoon almond or vanilla extract

zest of 1 lemon

1 Trader Joe's Gourmet Pie Crust (in the frozen-food section), defrosted (refreeze the remaining one for another use)

4 plums, sliced

2 tablespoons turbinado sugar, for garnish (optional)

handful of slivered almonds, for garnish (optional)

VEGETARIAN

Preheat the oven to 375°F. Place the almonds in a food processor and pulse to grind the nuts to a powder. Remove to a bowl and set aside. Place the butter and sugar in the processor and blend until light and thoroughly combined. Add one egg and process to combine. Add the second egg and repeat. Add the ground almonds and the flour, and process just until combined. Add the almond or vanilla extract and lemon zest and combine. Chill in the refrigerator for 30 minutes or in freezer 15 minutes.

Roll the pie dough with a rolling pin, if necessary to repair cracks. Place on a parchment-lined baking sheet. Spread the filling onto the center of the pie crust, leaving a 2-inch border of pastry uncovered. Arrange the plum slices in a pretty pattern over the top and fold the pastry edges in, on top of the filling, leaving the center of the filling exposed. Bake until puffed and golden, about 25 minutes. (If desired, sprinkle crunchy sugar, such as turbinado, or sliced almonds over the top of the tart in the last 5 minutes of baking.)

SERVES: 8
PREP TIME: 10 minutes, plus 15 to 30 minutes to chill
COOKING TIME: 25 minutes

BREAD PUDDING with BOURBON SAUCE

As my dear friend Bob would say, this rich dessert is "slap yo' momma good!"

BOURBON SAUCE:

1 egg

⅓ cup granulated sugar

⅓ cup brown sugar

¼ cup water

4 tablespoons butter

¼ cup bourbon

BREAD PUDDING:

8 cups bread cubes made from about eight-day-old croissants

½ cup raisins, Trader Joe's Golden Berry Blend, or chocolate chips

3 eggs

½ cup granulated sugar

⅓ cup brown sugar

2 cups milk

1 cup heavy cream

1 tablespoon vanilla

½ teaspoon cinnamon

VEGETARIAN

FOR THE BOURBON SAUCE: In a medium bowl, beat the egg with a fork to combine the white and yolk well. Set aside. In a small saucepan, combine the sugars, water, and butter. Bring to a simmer, and cook until the sugar is dissolved. Pour about a third of this mixture into the beaten egg, whisking rapidly as you pour. (This will help to prevent the eggs from scrambling.) Then return that mixture to the saucepan and cook over low heat, stirring, about 2 minutes, until sauce thickens. Remove the pan from the heat and stir in the bourbon. The bourbon sauce can be made several hours, or even a day, ahead and then refrigerated. (Rewarm before serving.)

FOR THE BREAD PUDDING: Preheat the oven to 325°F. Butter a 2-quart baking dish or about eight ramekins. Toss the bread with the raisins, berries, or chocolate chips in a large bowl. Whisk together the remaining ingredients and pour over the bread. Cover with plastic wrap and weigh down, if necessary, to immerse the bread in the egg mixture, or stir occasionally. Let stand 15 minutes.

Place the bread mixture into the prepared dish(es). Bake 30 minutes (for ramekins) to 1 hour (for 2-quart dish). When done, the top will be golden brown, and a knife inserted into the center should come out clean. Cool slightly before serving with bourbon sauce on top.

SERVES: 8
PREP TIME: 10 minutes
COOKING TIME: 30 to 60 minutes

CHERRY-BERRY CRISP

This smells heavenly as it bakes, and tastes even better, if that's possible.

2 (16-ounce) bags Trader Joe's Very Cherry Berry Blend (frozen berries with no strawberries)

¼ cup powdered sugar

½ cup Trader Joe's Buttermilk Pancake Mix

½ cup brown sugar

½ cup McCann's Quick Cooking Irish Oatmeal

¼ cup butter

½ cup nuts (hazelnuts, pecans, walnuts, or whatever you like)

about ½ cup Trader Joe's Greek Yogurt and maple syrup or honey (optional)

VEGETARIAN

Preheat the oven to 375°F. Combine the berries and powdered sugar in a 2-quart ovenproof casserole and set aside. In a food processor, combine the rest of the ingredients and pulse to combine coarsely. Place this mixture on top of the berries and bake until bubbly, about 30 minutes. Cool for 5 to 10 minutes before serving. Top individual servings with yogurt sweetened to taste with maple syrup or honey, if desired.

SERVES: 6
PREP TIME: 5 minutes
COOKING TIME: 30 minutes

You can vary the frozen fruit for different flavor combinations. Peaches (fresh or frozen) and some chopped crystallized ginger are terrific! I prefer not to use frozen strawberries because they tend to exude more water than other fruits.

MEYER LEMON RASPBERRY CLOUDS

Meyer lemons are less acidic than regular ones, and their skin is deeply fragrant. If your TJ's doesn't have them in stock, use regular lemons and a little more sugar or some agave syrup.

4 eggs

½ cup sugar

1 cup heavy cream

2 teaspoons Meyer lemon zest

½ cup Meyer lemon juice (from about 2 medium lemons)

1 pint raspberries

VEGETARIAN, GLUTEN-FREE

Preheat the oven to 325°F. Whisk the eggs and sugar together, and then whisk in the cream. Whisk in the lemon zest and juice. Place six ramekins (or custard cups) in a larger baking pan with a high rim, divide the lemon mixture evenly between the ramekins, and add a few raspberries to each ramekin. Place the baking pan in the oven. Fill the baking pan with warm water halfway up the sides of the ramekins. Bake for 30 to 40 minutes, or until set but still jiggly. Serve hot, warm, or chilled.

SERVES: 6
PREP TIME: 15 minutes
COOKING TIME: 40 minutes

MINI VANILLA WAFER CHEESECAKES

This recipe is just waiting to be played around with. Pop some berries in before you bake them, or maybe a little piece of caramel. Crushed gingersnaps would be great as the base, too.

12 Trader Joe's Organic Vanilla Wafer Cookies

½ cup sugar

2 eggs

8 ounces cream cheese, at room temperature

8 ounces mascarpone, at room temperature

1 teaspoon vanilla

zest of 1 lemon

Trader Jacque's Fleur de Sel Caramel Sauce, for garnish

VEGETARIAN

Preheat the oven to 325°F. Place paper liners in a 12-hole muffin pan and place a vanilla wafer in the bottom of each. With an electric mixer, combine the sugar and eggs, then add the cream cheese, mascarpone, vanilla, and lemon zest, and mix to combine. Pour over the vanilla wafers, dividing evenly. Bake until set, 20 to 25 minutes. Cool before serving. Top each mini-cheesecake with a drizzle of caramel sauce.

SERVES: 12
PREP TIME: 10 minutes
COOKING TIME: 25 minutes

HAZELNUT-PLUM BABY CAKES

I love the idea of individual cakes that bake up so quickly and taste so satisfying. Of course, you can use other fruit as well. I still mourn the discontinuation of the vanilla paste Trader Joe's used to carry, so I'm repeating my pleas for a write-in campaign!

2 plums, halved

¾ cup Trader Joe's Raw Oregon Hazelnuts (or Unsalted Dry Toasted Slivered Almonds)

½ cup butter

½ cup sugar

2 eggs

1 teaspoon vanilla extract or paste

⅓ cup flour

VEGETARIAN

Preheat the oven to 400°F. Place half a plum, cut side down, in each of four ovenproof ramekins. In a food processor, finely chop the hazelnuts (or almonds). Set aside. Place the butter and sugar in the food processor, and blend until smooth. Add the eggs, vanilla extract, flour, and the chopped nuts and pulse just until combined. Spoon the batter over the plums, dividing evenly among the ramekins. Smooth the surface and bake until golden, about 20 minutes.

SERVES: 4
PREP TIME: 10 minutes
COOKING TIME: 20 minutes

MAXI-MINI PEANUT BUTTER CUP COOKIES

I'm not much of a peanut butter girl, and there are a million candy bars on the shelf I'd scarf up before I ate a peanut butter cup. But these cookies have something special goin' on, and I've been known to eat several at a time.

3 ounces butter, at room temperature

¼ cup peanut butter

½ cup granulated sugar

⅓ cup dark brown sugar

1 egg

1 teaspoon vanilla

1 cup flour

pinch salt

⅛ teaspoon baking soda

1 cup Trader Joe's Mini Milk Chocolate Peanut Butter Cups

VEGETARIAN

Preheat the oven to 375°F. Line a baking sheet with parchment. With an electric mixer, beat the butter with the peanut butter until light, about 2 minutes. Add the granulated and brown sugar and beat to combine well. Add the egg and vanilla and mix well. With a rubber spatula or wooden spoon, stir in the flour, salt, and baking soda until just combined. Add the mini peanut butter cups and stir gently to distribute them well in the batter. Drop by spoonfuls onto the prepared baking sheet and bake until golden, about 12 minutes.

MAKES: 1½ dozens
PREP TIME: 10 minutes
COOKING TIME: 12 minutes

Consider making decadent ice cream sandwiches with these cookies and TJ's terrific vanilla ice cream.

PUMPKIN CRANBERRY CAKE with PUMPKIN BUTTER–MASCARPONE SLATHER

Terrific with a cup of tea in the afternoon or for a lunchbox treat.

1 (17.5-ounce) box Trader Joe's Pumpkin Bread & Muffin Mix

2 eggs

½ cup canola oil

1 cup cranberry juice

½ cup dried cranberries

1 (10-ounce) jar Trader Joe's Pumpkin Butter

1 (8-ounce) container mascarpone

honey and/or bourbon (optional)

VEGETARIAN

Preheat the oven to 350°F. Lightly oil an 8- or 9-inch cake pan, or spray it with baking spray. Place the pumpkin bread mix in a large bowl. In a small bowl, stir together the eggs, oil, and cranberry juice, then add this mixture to the pumpkin bread mix, stirring to combine. Stir in dried cranberries and pour the mixture into the prepared pan. Bake until a skewer or knife blade inserted in the center comes out clean, 30 to 40 minutes.

Stir together the pumpkin butter and mascarpone. Flavor with bourbon and/or sweeten with honey, if desired. Pipe or spoon a dollop of the fluffy sauce on each slice of cake to serve.

SERVES: 6
PREP TIME: 5 minutes
COOKING TIME: 40 minutes

Both the pumpkin butter and the pumpkin bread mix are seasonal, so be sure to hoard enough to last you through the year!

TART AUX TROIS NOIX

This tart is featured on all holiday dessert tables in our family. Use whatever nuts you love most, and add dried cherries, cranberries, or chopped dried apricots for a chewier texture.

1 Trader Joe's Gourmet Pie Crust (in the frozen-food section), defrosted (refreeze the remaining one for another use)

½ cup bittersweet chocolate, chopped (see note)

8 tablespoons unsalted butter

⅓ cup flavorful honey

2 tablespoons heavy cream

½ cup brown sugar

3 cups (total) hazelnuts, pecans, and walnuts, coarsely chopped

½ teaspoon vanilla

VEGETARIAN

Preheat the oven to 375°F. Roll out the pie dough and fit into an 8- or 9-inch pie pan or tart pan with a removable bottom. Cover the pastry with crinkled parchment and weigh it down with a layer of pie weights, uncooked rice, or dried beans. Place in the oven for 12 minutes. Carefully remove the parchment, with weights inside, and return pan to the oven for 5 to 10 minutes, until pastry is dry and golden. Scatter the chopped chocolate over the warm pastry and let sit for a moment, until it begins to melt from the heat of the pastry. Spread the chocolate evenly over the bottom of the pastry shell. In a medium saucepan, combine the butter, honey, cream, and brown sugar and bring to a boil, stirring. Boil 3 to 4 minutes, then stir in nuts and vanilla. Pour into pastry shell and bake 20 minutes.

SERVES: 8
PREP TIME: 15 minutes
COOKING TIME: 45 minutes

I like to use the Pound Plus Bittersweet Chocolate bar—you'll have plenty left over for another purpose (like eating!)

STICKY CARAMEL CAKELETS

Perfect for a rainy evening, this version of sticky toffee pudding is comfort in a ramekin. The zing of ginger keeps the dessert from being too stodgy and overly sweet.

5 tablespoons butter, divided

10 to 12 pitted medjool dates, chopped

1 cup water

1 teaspoon baking soda

3 tablespoons crystallized ginger, chopped

½ cup brown sugar

2 eggs, room temperature

2 teaspoons vanilla

1¼ cups flour

1 teaspoon baking powder

pinch of salt

1 jar Trader Jacques Fleur de Sel Caramel Sauce, warmed

VEGETARIAN

Preheat oven to 350°. Butter 8 individual ramekins or a 1½-quart soufflé dish with 1 tablespoon butter. Set on a baking sheet. Place the chopped dates in a small saucepan and cover with the water. Bring to a boil, and stir in the baking soda. Stir in the chopped ginger and set aside.

With a mixer, beat the remaining 4 tablespoons of butter and the brown sugar until well combined. Add the eggs and vanilla and beat until combined. Combine the flour, baking powder and salt, and add half of the mixture to the butter mixture. Stir to incorporate the flour. Add the date and ginger mixture and stir. Add the remaining flour mixture and stir just until incorporated.

Divide the batter between the ramekins (or pour into soufflé dish). Bake until slightly puffed and set—about 30 minutes for ramekins, and 50 to 60 minutes for a larger dish. Poke holes in the top of the cakes, and spoon some caramel over the top to seep inside the cakes.

SERVES: 8
PREP TIME: 15 minutes
COOKING TIME: 30 to 60 minutes

Dates want to stick to the knife when you chop them. Try lightly oiling your knife or kitchen scissors blades, or buy the dates pre-chopped.

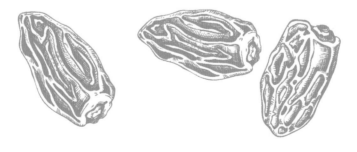

CONVERSIONS

VOLUM

U.S.	U.S. Equivalent	Metric
1 tablespoon (3 teaspoons)	½ fluid ounce	15 milliliters
¼ cup	2 fluid ounces	60 milliliters
⅓ cup	3 fluid ounces	90 milliliters
½ cup	4 fluid ounces	120 milliliters
⅔ cup	5 fluid ounces	150 milliliters
¾ cup	6 fluid ounces	180 milliliters
1 cup	8 fluid ounces	240 milliliters
2 cups	16 fluid ounces	480 milliliters

WEIGHT

U.S.	Metric
½ ounce	15 grams
1 ounce	30 grams
2 ounces	60 grams
¼ pound	115 grams
⅓ pound	150 grams
½ pound	225 grams
¾ pound	350 grams
1 pound	450 grams

TEMPERATURE

Fahrenheit (°F)	Celsius (°C)	Fahrenheit (°F)	Celsius (°C)
70°F	20°C	220°F	105°C
100°F	40°C	240°F	115°C
120°F	50°C	260°F	125°C
130°F	55°C	280°F	140°C
140°F	60°C	300°F	150°C
150°F	65°C	325°F	165°C
160°F	70°C	350°F	175°C
170°F	75°C	375°F	190°C
180°F	80°C	400°F	200°C
190°F	90°C	425°F	220°C
200°F	95°C	450°F	230°C

ACKNOWLEDGMENTS

Thanks to all the students and readers who've embraced the I Love Trader Joe's books over the past ten years. I still love hearing from you, letting me know that you are still using my recipes, which makes me ridiculously pleased.

Thanks to Ulysses Press for reaching out, long ago, and again recently. At first I thought "I can't write another TJ's book—I live far away and I no longer have a school full of recipe testers. That was a different lifetime ago." But friends and family encouraged me to look at the project from a new angle, and that's been a lot of fun.

To those friends and family, thanks beyond measure. Through all that's transpired since the first book came into the world, I've come to know what true friendship and support look like. I'm boundlessly blessed with a circle of people who have my back, lift me up, and make me laugh—never underestimate that gift! My grown children—wise and talented Kevin and his amazing wife Nicole, whom I think of as my new daughter, Brenna and her outstanding skills as the best poet-lawyer-daughter on Earth, and Matthew, who I hope is still proud of his mama, as he was in life—you are my everything. Ma.

As this book goes to print, the founder of Trader Joe's, Joe Coulombe, has passed away. Cheers and deep thanks to a bon vivant, a visionary, and a true leader.

ABOUT THE AUTHOR

© Patrice Dwyer www.imagesbypatrice.com

CHERIE MERCER TWOHY is a food writer, culinary tour leader, and unabashed Trader Joe's stockpiler. After 15 years of teaching thousands of students to fall in love with Trader Joe's, Cherie moved to a tiny town on the Oregon coast, where she sees whales from her window. She lives 60 miles from her closest TJ's but still makes frequent provisioning trips. With four I Love Trader Joe's books to her credit, she is currently at work on a novel about a cheese whisperer. She always carries a corkscrew and a cheese knife. She can be reached at cherie@ilovetraderjoes.com